The Stockbroker's Guide to Put and Call Option Strategies

LeRoy Gross

NEW YORK INSTITUTE OF FINANCE

**The Stockbroker's Guide
to Put and Call Option
Strategies**

© 1974 by the New York Institute of Finance

0–13–846725–0

10   9   8   7   6   5   4   3   2

**New York Institute of Finance
2 New York Plaza
New York, New York 10004**

To the women in my life

Eva
June
Linda
Paula

Contents

Introduction

At the time this book is being written, there exist in the United States two distinct markets for stock options on publicly traded securities. One market is the new Chicago Board Options Exchange, which began April 26, 1973. This exchange initially began trading in call options only on a limited number of New York Stock Exchange stocks. The list is being expanded periodically and eventually will probably exceed one hundred stocks. Put options are expected to be added as soon as it is practical to do so. The second option market is known as the over-the-counter option market, sometimes referred to as the New York option market. This market has been in existence for decades. In it, one can buy or sell call or put options on thousands of different securities. There are substantial differences in the option contracts offered in these two markets, and this book will outline the differences, the advantages, and the disadvantages of each. One significant difference should be noted here. In the initial months of the Chicago Board Options Exchange's existence, even though it dealt in call options only on a very small number of stocks, its average daily volume exceeded that of the over-the-counter option market, which has been in existence for many years and has the ability to provide options on thousands of stocks.

Perhaps at the time this book is published, there will be a third or maybe a fourth or fifth different option market. The American Stock Exchange has publicly announced interest in having option trading on its exchange. The PBW (Philadelphia, Baltimore, and Washington Stock Exchange) has also announced its intent to thoroughly investigate this vehicle as a method for stimulating business on its exchange. The National Stock Exchange is trying to develop a program for trading stock options. Even the prestigious New York Stock Exchange, under the direction of James Needham, President, has expressed its interest and is investigating the feasibility of trading stock options on the NYSE.

All this interest is in a little-known, much misunderstood investment vehicle—an option contract. Should some of these other interested exchanges develop an option business, it is quite conceivable that this particular vehicle will be to the securities industry of the seventies and beyond what the mutual fund was to the securities industry in the fifties and sixties.

One thing that seems to hold true is that strategies involving the use of options for both the buyer and the writer are substantially the same in either of the current option markets; and this will probably be the case in any new option markets that come into being. Of course, there will be differences in the terms of the contracts in each market, and each new exchange that begins trading in stock options will try to obtain some advantage over other options markets by seeking to make its particular contract unique in some special way. However, little will be done to change the basic concept of option contracts as to their inherent trading possibilities, protection possibilities, and income possibilities.

It is suggested that the reader try to understand this book *one chapter at a time* rather than read through the entire book and try to retain the information. Deeper understanding and longer retention will come by reviewing each chapter three or four times. That way, the knowledge the investor acquires will become increasingly valuable and accessible to him.

In the ensuing chapters, the letters *OTC* are used to designate over-the-counter, or New York, options and the letters *CBOE* to designate Chicago Board Options Exchange options.

I The OTC Option Market

1 The Registered Representative

Men and women who want a selling career enter the security sales field for three main reasons. The first is the attractiveness of *unlimited earning potential;* there is no ceiling on the amount of income that may be earned. The second is the *prestige* or distinction that is believed to go with the term *stockbroker* and the association with Wall Street. The third is the ability to be almost an *independent business person* without having the capital commitment required of most businesses.

Currently, most brokerage firms furnish office facilities, secretarial help, research aids, and so on, to aid their salesmen in attaining their income goals. Many firms also provide leads and maintain staffs of experts in various product areas to aid salesmen in obtaining accounts.

Those security salesmen who affiliate with member firms of the New York Stock Exchange, Inc., American Stock Exchange, Inc., and the National Association of Security Dealers, Inc. are called registered representatives. They must pass stringent examinations given by the National Association of Security Dealers and by the New York Stock Exchange.

Registered representatives, as well as other security salesmen, are also known by various other terms, such as account executives, customers' men, and stockbrokers. Regardless of name, they all should have certain knowledge and skill requirements in common. These include: (1) Knowledge of securities laws, regulations, and procedures; (2) knowledge of investment products sold by their firms; (3) skill in determining clients' wants and needs and in constructing investment programs to meet them; and (4) personal skill in selling and servicing clients' accounts.

Registered representatives of New York Stock Exchange member firms must go through a six-month training period before they are permitted to deal with the public. During this training period, they must acquaint themselves with the various rules and regulations covering their security transactions with clients. One of the most important rules with which they must be well acquainted is Rule 405, which governs the opening of accounts for clients as well as the manner in which clients' affairs are handled. This rule has come to be known as the "know your customer" rule. Excerpts from this rule are as follows:

Rule 405

Diligence as to Accounts

Every member organization is required through a general partner, a principal executive officer or a person or persons designated under the provisions of Rule 342(b) (1) (2342) to

(1) Use due diligence to learn the essential facts relative to every customer, every order, every cash or margin account accepted or carried by such organization and every person holding power of attorney over any account accepted or carried by such organization.

Supervision of Accounts

(2) Supervise diligently all accounts handled by registered representatives of the organization.

Approval of Accounts

(3) Specifically approve the opening of an account prior to or promptly after the completion of any transaction for the account of or with a customer, provided, however, that in the case of branch offices, the opening of an account for a customer may be approved by the manager of such branch office but the action of such branch office manager shall within a reasonable time be approved by a general partner, officer or designated person approving the opening of the account shall, prior to giving his approval, be personally informed as to the essential facts relative to the customer and to the nature of the proposed account and shall indicate his approval in writing on a document which is a part of the permanent records of his office or organization.

After a registered representative has completed his training program and his salary or "drawing" salary is discontinued, he has to depend on obtaining commissions from clients in order to earn his living. Merrill Lynch, Pierce, Fenner & Smith, *alone,* among major New York Stock Exchange firms, pays account executives a nondrawing salary on a continuing basis. This salary is augmented by periodic bonuses. The salary plus bonuses reportedly approximates 25 percent of commissions produced by the account executive.

In earning commissions from clients, the registered representative has to be careful that trades in clients' accounts are made in line with their particular stated investment objectives. In order to avoid possible law suits and disciplinary action by the regulatory bodies, he has to be very careful that he does not *churn* an account. He can make himself and his firm liable should losses occur [1] and the commissions generated be deemed excessive in relation to the amount of capital and the customer's objectives.

Many registered representatives feel caught sometimes in what appears to be a conflict of interest between the client's welfare and the representative's need to earn a living from commissions earned from his customers' accounts. This conflict is intensified many times by the pressure placed on the registered representative by the employer firm to produce commissions at a certain minimum level. Additional pressure is often brought by the client's desire to earn profits, many times, as quickly as possible. Of course, there is always present the natural greed that is inherent in most investors (and commission salesmen).

Although many investors think and talk about the long-term outlook for their security purchases, most are really interested in obtaining profits in a very short term—usually six months to a year in their stock purchases. An old Wall Streeter once defined *traders* as *security purchasers whose stocks rose in value—investors* as *security purchasers whose stocks declined in value!*

How can the registered representative resolve this conflict? How can he do his very best to advise clients in their profit search and at the same time earn reasonable commission income for himself and conduct his business on the highest ethical planes? One avenue that can help solve these issues is to become more knowledgeable in Wall Street's most sophisticated areas—*margin trading* and *option trading.*

---

[1] Even if there are profits, an account can still be churned—so say the courts.

2 Understanding Margin

Unfortunately, most registered representatives do not really understand margin account transactions well enough to correctly advise clients in margin usage. Knowing and understanding margin regulations and requirements can be a great asset to a security salesman in developing a large clientele for the firm and himself. However, there is *no easy way* to do this. Hard work and diligent study are required to learn the facts concerning margin and its many possible applications—facts and strategies, that, once learned, might help increase clients' assets (and, in some cases, *decrease their assets*) or protect their profits and capital.

Gaining an understanding of current margin regulations and uses can be of invaluable help to registered representatives in assisting current clients and in obtaining new clients. The margin-knowledgeable broker stands head and shoulders above less informed competitors. It must be realized, however, that the margin rules governing stock and bond trading are very complex. Understanding them does not, in itself, guarantee sales success for account executives. Once these rules and regulations have been mastered, the representative must learn how to apply them. Then, he must develop the ability to *convey* this information to the client or prospect in a manner that makes it *easy* for him to understand, and, of course, then *put to use* in his own market transactions.

This book attempts to present *margin understanding* and *utilization* in as simple a manner as possible for easy comprehension. In so doing, however, some of the very complex rules and regulations, as well as applications, are *purposely* omitted. The serious student can gain this knowledge from other publications, such as Robert Rittereiser's *Margin Regulations and Practices,* New York Institute of Finance, 1973.

Margin is a term used in the brokerage community to indicate credit. An investor *on margin* has simply borrowed funds from his broker. The amount owed to the broker is called the *debit balance.* In order to protect his loan, the broker who lends money to an investor is required to obtain collateral from the borrower in the form of cash or securities.

Should investors borrow from brokerage firms? How much can be borrowed? Who governs the amount of loans and their terms? Many questions like these are asked by investors everywhere. The sincere, success-oriented registered representative will learn the answers to such questions, plus many other significant margin facts.

In seeking profits in the stock market, or in bond, commodity, or real estate transactions, one constantly comes in contact with the word *leverage*. The awesome power that can be applied through the use of leverage is probably the number one reason given by people who purchase securities with borrowed money. Correctly leveraged decisions magnify gains on actual cash or collateral deposited by the borrowing investor. Of course, the sword of leverage has two edges —people who use leverage investments to seek gains for themselves *must be constantly aware* that the leverage can work against, as well as for, them. Their loss potential when leverage is employed is magnified, as is their profit potential.

Currently, the initial margin deposits for stock purchases is set by the Federal Reserve Board at 65 percent. (The New York Stock Exchange also requires a $2,000 minimum initial equity deposit in a margin account when funds are loaned to a client.)

Using this percentage, let's look at two examples of leverage —one working out favorably for an investor, and one showing an adverse result. Let's assume, in the first example, that an investor wishing to employ leverage buys 100 shares of ZYX at 40. By depositing 65 percent of the purchase price to meet the *minimum initial requirement,* he needs to invest only $2,600 of his funds. Assume that ZYX advances from 40 to 53, and he then sells 100 shares at 53. On this transaction, he will show a $1,300 gain on his $2,600 initial cash deposit. This gain represents a 50 percent gain on *his investment* in a stock that moved upward 32.5 percent. (The 50 percent gain does not include commissions to buy and sell and interest that must be paid on the debit balance owed to the lending broker.) Had this same stock declined, however, from the purchase price of 40 to a level of 27 and the decision was made to sell the 100 shares at 27, a $1,300 loss would have been incurred. This loss represents a 50 percent loss of the $2,600 original capital commitment that occurred on a stock price fall of 32.5 percent. Thus, leverage can work two ways!

Another reason for borrowing money from brokers is the feature involving a *no-repayment-date loan!* This attractive service generally is not available through banks or savings and loan institutions. In addition to the no-repayment-date feature, the borrower *is not re-*

quired to make any regular installment payments to repay or reduce the loan. What other lenders can you name that allow terms like these?

The no-repayment-date feature, although very attractive, can be fraught with danger. The investor should be made aware that if the value of securities on deposit with the broker *declines substantially,* the broker will require *additional funds or collateral* to protect his loan. This risk is *real.*

Once having opened a general margin account, many investors like the ease with which they can borrow money by simply calling the broker and having him issue a check for whatever available amount their collateral value permits. *No additional papers need to be signed,* nor a trip made from the house to the bank—perhaps in inclement weather—to fill out detailed forms to obtain a loan. Yes, margin accounts are attractive from this point of view, too.

And, of course, many investors with substantial accounts *like* the fact that at most large firms there is *no charge* (currently) for record-keeping services such as receipt and disbursement of dividends; also, *no charge* is made for the safe-keeping of their securities. At the end of each calendar year, investors generally receive from their brokerage firms a single, very simple statement for tax purposes of *all dividends received* and *all interest charged* during the calendar year. These attractive features, too, can help encourage investors to establish margin accounts.

Establishing margin accounts with exchange member firms is a comparatively simple matter in most cases. The registered representative must obtain and then *verify* certain information about the prospective client, including age, employment, income, bank reference, residence, investment objective, and so on. In addition, the client is required to sign a margin agreement, and in most cases, a loan consent form, as well. The margin agreement does two important things. It enables a lender to take whatever steps necessary to protect his loan should adverse market conditions affect the market value of the securities purchased (or sold short). The loan consent [1] form allows a lender to simply loan out the securities involved.[2] This loan of customers' securities, however, involves *no*

---

[1] The loan consent form also authorizes the broker to use securities in the customer's margin account as collateral for a broker's loan from a bank should the firm need to borrow money to lend to margin customers.

[2] On a temporary basis, to facilitate settlement of transactions by short sellers or by firms that have failed to receive the stock from their selling customers by the settlement date.

additional risk or loss of ownership on the part of the person depositing the collateral.

Who should use "borrowed money" to buy securities? Investors who are aggressive and who fully understand the risks as well as rewards in using leverage are normally the ones who use borrowed funds in their security transactions. Great care must be taken by the registered representative to see that margin accounts are properly opened and that the transactions made are suitable in accordance with Rule 405 of the NYSE. There are many long-term investors as well as active traders who utilize margin in attempting to reach their investment objectives. However, suitability always must be the governing factor in soliciting business of this type.

In explaining to clients and prospects the risks, as well as the advantages, of using borrowed money in their search for profits, the registered representative must be very careful to explain the possibilities of a *sell-out*. If security values in an account decline substantially, the lending broker will notify the client that more funds or securities must be deposited in order to protect the loan already made. Should the additional funds or securities *not* be deposited as requested, the lending broker *may sell* the securities in the account to prevent the firm's capital from being placed at risk. *This can and does happen* in severely declining markets. This prospect, of course, *must not be minimized* to clients.

Interest charges are going to be incurred by the client using borrowed funds. Normally, these interest charges are at rates related to the borrowing cost of the broker, as well as to the activity and size of the account and the amount of money owed. New York Stock Exchange rules require that the lending broker charge interest at least one-half of one percent *above* his borrowing cost as a *minimum charge*. Many exchange firms charge *more than the minimum* to small debit balance holders or to accounts that are inactive in nature.

Transactions That Can Only Be Made in Margin Accounts

There's a misconception prevalent in Wall Street that margin accounts are *only for sophisticated, aggressive investors.* Knowledgeable and alert registered representatives should understand that this is *not necessarily true.* Simply having a margin account *does not* mean that a client *has to owe* money to the broker. *Certain transactions are required to be margin transactions* under rules formulated by the New York Stock Exchange or the Federal Reserve Board. Making use of these transactions can be the province of *conservative investors* who would never, ever, consider owing money to anyone or paying interest.

What are these transactions? Sometimes, buying and writing put and call options, although some firms do allow cash account purchases of puts and calls. Another is the use of *short-against-the-box* transactions. Let's examine in more detail the various kinds of transactions that can be consummated in a margin account as well as the most popular type of securities involved in margin transactions.

Short Sales

All *short sales,* by regulation, have to be executed in a margin account. "Now, exactly what is a short sale?" is a question frequently asked of registered representatives. A short sale [3] is a sale of securities that will not be delivered by the seller within the normal settlement time. A short sale has to be *arranged* by having the broker borrow the security that is being sold short to deliver to the buyer. The short seller hopes to profit from a *price decline* in the security he shorts. He hopes and believes that he will have the opportunity to buy the securities at a later date at a *lower price* and then effect a delivery. If the short seller is correct in his judgment, he earns a profit. If he is wrong, he may have to buy the security sold short at a higher price and thereby *sustain a loss.* The Internal Revenue Service must view regular short selling with a jaundiced eye, as it *always taxes a regular short sale profit as a short-term capital gain!* In other words, no matter how long one has remained in a regular short position, whenever it is closed the profit earned can only be counted as a short-term capital gain.

Short against the Box

This practice can be used by even the most conservative investor and is much different from a regular short sale. Many times, an investor holds securities that have increased in value, and he would dearly like to take advantage of the current price of the securities by selling. And yet, if he has previously earned profits or other income, he may hate to incur additional capital gains in the current taxable year. A knowledgeable registered representative can offer a

---

[3] A short sale of a listed stock can only be executed on an *uptick.*

solution in this situation by having the client deposit his securities with the brokerage firm, which, at the client's request, can then sell a like amount of these securities *short against the box*. By using this procedure, the client *locks* in the current price of the stock. He then may remain in this position as long as he wants.

Most commonly, however, the client waits until a new tax year begins and then instructs his broker to close out the box transaction by delivering the securities he originally deposited. This effectively pushes the capital gains earned by the client into a different taxable year in which his income may be lower and, therefore, the taxes on the gains will be lower. This short-against-the-box transaction is a perfectly legal tax maneuver, and it can help a registered representative to gain the respect of many clients and prospects.

Please note that a profit earned when delivering securities to close a short against the box can be a *long-term* capital gain *if* the short is executed *after* a six-month holding period has been established for the securities that are used to close the transaction. Also note that short-against-the-box transactions do not subject the investor to risk, as he owns and can deliver the securities. The investor in this situation also surrenders the potential for further gain by locking himself into the price of the short-against-the-box sale.

"What Securities Are Purchased on Margin?"

What securities can be purchased in margin accounts is fundamental knowledge for the successful registered representative. Basic categories include: stock exchange listed stocks; tax-exempt municipal bonds; stock exchange listed convertible bonds; stock exchange listed nonconvertible bonds; and many over-the-counter stocks. Most over-the-counter stocks are *not* marginable, but a constantly updated list of those that are can be furnished to an investor by any New York Stock Exchange brokerage firm. Some New York Stock Exchange firms accept margin purchases of government bonds as well.

From time to time, the NYSE may require *100 percent cash* payment for listed stocks bought or sold short on the exchange. This condition usually arises when the action of the listed security has caused the exchange to eliminate credit transactions temporarily. Additionally, many exchange firms require full cash payment for stocks that are very low in price—some firms for stocks under five dollars. It's very important for registered representatives to know these facts and to transmit them to clients and prospects. *Failure to know and understand basic margin regulations and rules can not only cause the loss of a client to a more knowledgeable competitor, it can also render the registered representative and the firm liable to litigation.*

"Who Establishes Margin Requirements?"

This is a common question from clients and prospects. Every registered representative should be reasonably familiar with who does set the initial deposit requirements for various security purchases on margin. To make it easier to understand and explain, the following information should, perhaps, be committed to memory.

There are *three sets* of margin requirements to be met by an investor. One is set by the Federal Reserve Board via Regulation T. Another is set by the New York Stock Exchange, and the third is set by the New York Stock Exchange member firm (called *the house*). The fact to remember is that for any given margin security, the *highest requirement of these three is the one the margin user must comply with.*

The Federal Reserve Board changes the minimum initial deposit requirements for credit purchases periodically, after reviewing market activity in a particular issue. In September 1973, these requirements are:

1. *For listed stock purchases,* 65% of the purchase price
2. *For listed convertible bonds,* 50% of the current market price
3. *For listed nonconvertible bonds,* 30% of the purchase price [4]
4. *For marginable OTC stocks,* 65% of the purchase price

Author's note: in January 1974, the Federal Reserve Board lowered the initial margin requirement to 50%.

The New York Stock Exchange requires a $2,000 minimum deposit to make a credit purchase, with these two exceptions: (1) If the Federal Reserve Board or the house requirement for the particular security purchase the customer contemplates comes to more than $2,000, *the customer must meet the highest requirement;* and (2) if the proposed purchase will cost less than $2,000, *the customer must pay in full, but he need not deposit more than the actual purchase price for the particular transaction.*

For regular short sales of marginable stocks, the current Federal Reserve Board minimum deposit requirement is 65 percent of the short sale proceeds. Note that credit balances created by short

---

[4] Reg T 220.8 sets maximum loan value to be set by creditor. NYSE requires a minimum of 25%. Most firms adhere to 30%.

sales cannot be utilized by the investor until the short position is covered.

Many times, the house requirement is *higher* than the New York Stock Exchange or Federal Reserve Board minimums. Sometimes this high requirement is due to the volatility of the security or to a concentration in the security that could possibly affect the marketability. As stated before, the customer must meet the highest initial deposit requirement, be it FRB, NYSE, or house.

Margin Maintenance

In marketing the concept of using margin to potential clients, one must be familiar with what is known as *margin maintenance.*

The New York Stock Exchange has established requirements that an account maintain a *minimum* of 25 percent equity in the account. Equity is defined for stock owners as the customer's ownership interest in the account. This equity is determined by subtracting the debit balance from the current market value of the securities in the account. Should security values fall to this minimum level (again, individual firms may require higher minimums than this), the broker will "call" for more money or securities to protect the loan. Every registered representative should be familiar with his particular firm's maintenance margin requirements.

Risk-Reducing Transactions Available in Margin Accounts

By having a margin account, a client is able to participate in many *risk-reducing techniques* that open additional avenues to him in his profit search. Some of these techniques are as follows.

Arbitrage Transactions

This practice involves almost simultaneous purchases and sales of the same security, or substantially identical securities, in different markets in order to profit from a price differential.

Reverse Warrant Hedges

This is the practice of selling short warrants of a particular issue while maintaining, at the same time, a long position in the stock of the warrant issuer.

Warrant Hedges

This practice involves the short selling of stock collateralized by warrants, which, upon exercise, will establish a long position in the stock sold short.

Convertible Hedges

This risk-limiting practice involves the short selling of common stock against a long position in convertible bonds or convertible preferred, which, upon conversion, will establish a long position in the stock sold short.

Purchasing Option Contracts

These transactions are purchases made to seek speculative profits with predetermined risk, to insure profits, or to protect a stock position. Some member firms permit the purchasing of puts and calls to take place in a cash account as well as in the margin account.

Issuing Option Contracts

This is a practice involving receipt of option buyers' premiums in an attempt to generate above-average income for the writer of the contract. Under certain circumstances, and with some member firms, option contracts may be issued in a cash account. Most firms, however, permit this activity only in a margin account.

3 Strategy for OTC Call Option Buyers

Once a registered representative has become familiar with margin terms, uses, and applications, his attention is often directed to the buying of option contracts—puts and calls, as they are commonly known. Recent rules established by the Federal Reserve Board allow put and call options to be purchased in a cash account as well as in a *general margin account*. However, some New York Stock Exchange member firms restrict cash account purchases of options to institutions. Payment terms for put and call options vary from firm to firm. Some demand payment the same day of purchase. Others allow one-day settlements, and others allow from three to five days.

In general, option buying has *three specific objectives*. One is the *seeking of large gains* over a specified, and usually short, period of time. The second is for *short-term trading purchases*. The third usage is for *insurance purposes*. Each of these will be discussed in detail.

There are really *only two contracts* in the world of stock options—the put contract and the call contract. There are many combinations of these contracts, however, and we will familiarize the reader with the terms of these variations and the names they go by. The most popular contract by far, the one that represents as much as 80 to 90 percent of all option purchases, is the call option.

The registered representative seeking to build his business should try to gain all the option knowledge he can, as this useful tool is gaining in investor acceptance. Clients, of course, will be interested in the *many advantages* of the call option. The two primary advantages are the *relatively unlimited profit potential* combined with *absolute predetermined limited risk* (which can be, of course, 100 percent of the premium paid).

There are two main markets in the United States for trading option contracts. One is the over-the-counter option market, often referred to as the New York market or the OTC market. The second option marketplace is the new Chicago Board Options Exchange, which came into being April 26, 1973.

There are many differences between the two markets. Each

has advantages and disadvantages over the other. These differences, advantages and disadvantages, will be discussed in the following chapters.

Simply defined, the call option is a contract that gives the holder the right to purchase 100 shares of a stock at a fixed price for a specified time period, adjusted according to the terms of the contract. Most people who purchase call option contracts, and most brokers who recommend them, are generally seeking large future profits within the particular time period of the option contract.

A good rule of thumb for OTC call option buyers to follow in their search for these large profits is to envision the *possible tripling* or more of the call option premium. Assume, for example, that stock XYZ (not listed on the Chicago Board Options Exchange) is selling in the marketplace at a price of approximately $40 per share and that an investor is interested in buying a call option on XYZ in search of long-term capital gain. Assume that he obtains a quotation for a six-month, ten-day call on this particular stock at 40 and is informed that the premium required to buy this call option is approximately $600.

Before *committing* his funds to this purchase, the speculator should be able to envision a price move for this particular stock from the $40 level to possibly $58 or higher within his chosen time period. If the underlying stock does not appear to offer the opportunity for this price advancement within the time period, then perhaps this call should not be purchased.

If this practice of envisioning a tripling or more of the call premium during the life of the contract were followed by OTC call buyers, *and if* their judgment proved right *only once out of every three options bought* (assuming the three option premiums were approximately equal), the OTC call buyer could break about even on all his option purchases by *one right judgment*. In other words, he would only have to be right one-third of the time.

If his judgment of stock price moves was correct *more than* one out of three times, he might earn substantial profits. Too often, however, OTC call buyers are not properly educated as to the risk/reward evaluation of their OTC call options; therefore, many are not successful in their OTC call-buying program even if right more than 33 percent of the time.

In purchasing OTC call options, one is faced with the problem of which time period represents the best value for the money spent. This is a legitimate issue, as new OTC call options that run from twenty-one days to as long as thirteen months are available to buyers.

Registered representatives would do well to advise clients to purchase OTC call contracts for *either* six months and ten days or one year. These two time periods generally represent the *best value for the OTC call option buyer.*

Sometimes, the greed inherent in many clients and brokers leads them to purchase 35-day, 65-day, and 95-day OTC call contracts. In making these short time-period purchases, the speculator is trying to save a relatively small amount of premium dollars and is forced to expect a price movement in his favor within this compressed time span. Sometimes, these short time-period purchases are made because the customer wants to spend fewer dollars and incur less risk, and sometimes they are made because the registered representative tries to generate commissions at a more rapid rate.

However, experience seems to prove that the customer's *best profit chance,* overall, lies in the purchase of the six-month, ten-day and one-year contracts. With the over-six-month contract, the customer has the possibility of being able to resell the contract after the six-month period of time has elapsed, thereby obtaining the *benefit of a long-term capital gain* should his judgment prove right. Second, he has *more time available for a price move to occur in his favor* —a move that might easily regain his premium, show him a profit, or reduce his loss.

The financial media do *not* run OTC option tables that reflect current prices being paid and received for OTC options, although, of course, such listings are printed daily for stocks and CBOE trades. Option dealers' ads in the financial papers usually feature "special" options that are in the dealers' inventories. These "special" options reflect prices available to buyers, not the prices writers can receive.

Many OTC call option buyers, as well as brokers, aren't familiar with prices they can expect to pay for varying periods of time and for many different stocks. A rule-of-thumb gauge can help to estimate the cost of OTC call options.

Stocks usually fall into three main categories: *high volatility, medium volatility,* and *low volatility.* If you can place a stock in one of these categories, the following guidelines will allow you to estimate the approximate cost of six-month, ten-day OTC calls.

1. OTC call options for six months, ten days on highly volatile listed stocks usually cost the buyer 15 to 20% of the current market price of the stock.

2. Six-month, ten-day OTC call options on medium-volatility listed stocks usually cost the buyer 10 to 14% of the current market price of the stock.

3. Six-month, ten-day OTC call options on listed stocks of low volatility and high quality usually cost the buyer 8 to 10% of the current market price of the stock.

4. Six-month, ten-day OTC call options on listed *low-priced* stocks, whether of high volatility or not, generally command premiums of about 25% of the current market price, due in part to the higher commission cost to the writer of the option.

5. Six-month, ten-day OTC call options on marginable over-the-counter stocks usually cost the buyer from 25 to 30% of the asked price of the stock.

Of course, there are exceptions to these guidelines, but in general, they hold true.

Registered representatives should also know the cost relationships among 95-day OTC call options, six-month, ten-day OTC call options, and one-year OTC call options. Once the six-month, ten-day call price is known, another rule-of-thumb guide can be applied to determine the approximate cost of a 95-day call option and a one-year call option on the same stock. The 95-day OTC call option will generally cost the buyer approximately *one-third less* than the cost of a six-month, ten-day OTC call option. Conversely, a one-year OTC call option will generally cost the buyer approximately 50 percent more than the price asked for a six-month, ten-day OTC call. In the final analysis, the factors that determine the price of any OTC call-option contract are *length of time of the option, the volatility of the stock,* and the *availability of the stock.*

In seeking OTC call-option purchases from clients and prospects, it is easy for a registered representative to get enthusiastic over the many attractive advantages that accrue to the holder of calls. Let's take a careful look at some of these advantages.

Most important, perhaps, is the *risk limitation.* A call buyer can *never* lose more than the premium he paid for his contract. He can lose all of it, but the extent of his risk is predetermined. He can sleep at night. He can have *peace of mind,* knowing that no matter how poorly the stock performs in the marketplace, his *loss can not increase.* Combined with this predetermined loss feature is the relatively *unlimited profit potential* that exists. Who knows how high a stock may rise in a given period of time?

Let's look at a positive and a negative example of an OTC call-option purchase. Assume an OTC call is bought on XYZ at 40, for six months and ten days, for a premium cost of $600 to the buyer. Assume that the stock, within the period of time, declines to $20 a share. The buyer will lose $600, although the *stock declined 50 percent* in value, or $2,000 on 100 shares. The $600 loss to the OTC call-option buyer, of course, will be mitigated to some extent by the tax relief he will get by claiming his loss as a tax-deductible capital loss—either a short-term capital loss if he held the contract less than six months, or a long-term capital loss if he held it over six months.

On the other hand, had this same stock at 40 risen to 60 within the time frame of six months and ten days, the OTC call-option buyer would have been able to dispose of his contract for $2,000, *less commissions incurred* for *purchase* of the stock at $40 and *sale* of the stock at $60. The investor in our example would have more than tripled his investment *after* payment of commission expenses.

Put and call dealers, as well as most New York Stock Exchange firms, are willing to purchase profitable OTC call options for the difference between strike price and market price. Commissions will be charged, but generally, *no value will be paid for any remaining time.*

Brokers who advise clients in the purchase of call options should be aware that there are two methods with which to seek profits through buying OTC call options. One is the *buy-and-pray method.* This technique is probably the one most employed by most clients and brokers, simply because they are not aware of the second method.

The *buy-and-pray method* involves purchasing the OTC call option, then holding it to the end of the time period. The investor prays that the underlying stock rises in value enough within the time period so that the option can then be resold to obtain the benefit of a long-term capital gain (if the option has been held over six months), as well as the return of the buyer's premium and the covering of his commission expenses.

This would be wonderful *if* the stock rose in value and stayed up near its peak just to accommodate the buyer of the OTC call. Most of the time, this does not occur. Many times, shortly after buying an OTC call, the investor joyfully observes a price rise in the stock. Since a long time remains in the contract life, no action is taken other than to "hope." The price rise is then followed by a price fall, and the buyer finds himself with a worthless option which he will have to claim as a capital loss tax deduction.

Knowledgeable brokers alert clients to the profit possibilities in the *trade-against method.* Ask any potential investor if he would like to make riskless trades in the stock market long or short and have an unlimited chance to earn profits, and I'm sure the reply will be a resounding "Yes!" But how do you do it? Is it ever done? The trade-against option method often allows an investor to make *riskless* trades in the stock market. Let's examine how this occurs.

Go back to our previous example. An OTC call option for six months and ten days is purchased on XYZ at 40 for $600. One month after the purchase of the call, XYZ rises to 50. The call-option buyer, at this point, is joyous. The broker who recommended the purchase of the call is also pleased. At this point, the client can sell—and the alert broker perhaps should recommend this action —100 shares of XYZ *short* at around the $50 price. He will, of course, have to put up the necessary collateral to margin the short sale, but he would be in a *riskless position.*

What could happen to the stock sold short at 50? Well, in the period remaining in the option life, the stock could go higher—or lower.

Let's assume that the stock sold short at 50 does the unexpected; violates most chart patterns, continues *straight up,* and *never comes below* the 50 price within the remaining life of the option. In this case, at the end of the option period, the call buyer would exercise his right to call for the stock at 40. He could use that stock to close out his short sale and would receive $1,000 from his broker, less commissions on the short sale at 50 and the stock purchase at 40. This would enable him to recover his premium cost, completely pay for his commission expense, and return to the investor a *profit* of approximately 50 percent on his premium risk investment. That's if the *worst* happened—the stock made a straight-up move after being shorted.

But what if the stock declines? Suppose a stock, after being shorted at 50, declines to 40. Well, the investor can buy 100 shares at the open market at 40 and use that 100 shares to close out his short sale. He will obtain a profit of $1,000 before commission expenses and still have *ownership* of his call option! It hasn't been used at this point, except to insure the short sale. Perhaps the stock will rise in price again and can be shorted again *without risk.*

There is no limit to how many trades against an option one can make within a specified time period; there have been instances of 10, 12, or as many as 14 trades within a six-month period. And in *Getting Rich with OPM (Other People's Money),* Paul Sarnoff tells of 27 trades within a year's time against a single option. Moreover, *all* trades closed out at a profit.

A *good rule* for the registered representative to suggest, in recommending the trade-against method to OTC call-option buyers, is *to close any short sale only at a profit to the option holder.*

In other words, if the client sells stock short with the protection of his option, he should *only cover* that short sale with a stock *purchase below* the short sale price. If the stock, after having been shorted, continues up . . . well, through exercise of the call, the premium, in full or in part, will be recovered, as well as expenses, and (with facts similar to our example) no loss, large or small, will be incurred.

If this practice is followed, what *will* occur is that the investor will gain trading profits with the protection of the option. *His risk will always be held in check and limited.* This will help avoid compliance problems, keep clients cheerful, and forestall having to guess about the stock market price of the individual stock.

An easy trap to fall into sometimes is to make a short sale with the protection of a call option and see the stock go up a couple of points and "feel" that it could go higher. The temptation exists to cover the short sale at a *loss.* Many investors have succumbed to this temptation, only to watch the stock fall back after the short sale has already been covered at a loss. This is a danger that should, and can, be avoided by the knowledgeable option broker. *Don't* try to *guess* the market. Use your call option as insurance. Let your client sleep at night with his mind free from worry. Complete trades against OTC call options at *profits* or *premium recovery only.* Then you will have *satisfied clients* and will be well along the road to success.

4 | OTC Option Contract Adjustments

OTC call-option buyers are going to want to know what happens when cash dividends, rights, warrants, stock dividends, or stock splits occur in the stock on which they hold OTC call options. This is only natural, and the broker must be familiar with how these occurrences affect the option contract.

Cash Dividends

If a stock goes ex a cash dividend within the life of the option contract, the contract price will be *reduced* by the amount of this cash dividend whenever the OTC call contract is exercised. In other words, the holder of the OTC call is entitled to call for the stock at the striking price *less* any cash dividends that have gone ex within that specified time period. OTC put options are also similarly reduced by any ex dividends that occur in the life of the contract.

Rights and Warrants

If any rights or warrants are issued and the stock goes ex rights or ex warrants during the holding period of an option, the striking price, upon exercise, will be *reduced* by an amount equal to the price at which the *first* sale of the rights or warrants is made on the day that particular stock sells ex rights or ex warrants.

Stock Dividends and Stock Splits

If a stock dividend or stock split occurs in a stock specified in an option contract, an adjustment is made to reflect the additional stock that would be involved on the exercise of the option. For instance, if an option holder held a call on 100 XYZ at 30, and XYZ split two for one, the call, when exercised, would give the option holder the right to call for 200 shares of XYZ at a total price of $3,000 (excluding, of course, commissions). In other words, the call holder is entitled to any additional shares of stock that go ex from a stock split or a stock dividend that occurs within the contract time-period.

5 Uses of OTC Call Options

Many option buyers purchase OTC call options on stocks that pay high dividends in order to benefit from a lower striking price in the event that the option is exercised.

A little-known use for call options is the *insurance* use. Call options can, many times, be used to *insure stock market profits*. Investors often find themselves on the horns of a dilemma. For example, suppose an investor has a stock purchased at $10 a share that is now selling in the market at $50 per share. He would like to take the money out of the stock—perhaps to use it elsewhere—yet he is afraid to sell too soon. He thinks perhaps the stock will go a lot higher, and by selling he will miss out on additional profits. He says to himself, "Look what this stock has done for me already. If I had surrendered to the temptation to sell earlier in the stock's move, I would not be sitting with this fine paper profit. Also, if I sell now, I incur a substantial tax on the gain."

One way out of this particular dilemma is to simply sell the stock at the current price of approximately $50—by doing so, the profit from $10 to $50 is accepted and established—then, *immediately* purchase a call option on the stock at the $50 level with *part* of the proceeds derived from the sale. This way, the client or investor will have the bulk of his money out of the stock that has risen so greatly in value, and he can use these funds elsewhere or isolate them from market risk by depositing them in a bank or by purchasing treasury bills. In this situation, the investor still *retains an interest* in the future price rise of the stock. Should the stock go upward from $50 to $100 per share in the life of his option, he still is a beneficiary, because he has the right to buy the stock at $50 through his call option.

Should the stock decline from $50 back to $10, the investor will lose his call option premium, which he considers as an insurance policy expense that protected his profit. The bulk of his gain plus his original investment will have been removed from this particular stock.

Much business awaits the registered representative who understands this aspect of call options. Many investors throughout the country would love to know this particular feature, and the ambitious RR should be prepared to suggest it to appropriate clients.

Another use for the call option is to *average down*. Often, an investor buys a stock, believing it, of course, to be a real value at the time of purchase—an investment that holds capital-gain possibilities that will, hopefully, be realized over the six- to twelve-month period ahead. After purchase, however, the stock may decline in value due to any of several factors. At this point, the typical investor usually begins to ask himself, or perhaps his broker, the following questions: Should he hold on to the stock, hoping for recovery? Should he buy more of the stock at the now lower price? Should he just sell the stock and give up hope of recovery, just accept the loss? Or, should he buy a six-month, ten-day (or longer) call option for a small fraction of his original investment?

The knowledgeable investor often follows the call-option approach. Suppose he has purchased 100 shares of a stock, at $40 per share. For whatever reason, he has continued to remain long down to a current level of $20 per share. Rather than buy another 100 shares at the new, lower level, which would require $2,000, he can purchase a call option. At the $20 level, a six-month, ten-day call option might be available for a premium of about $300.

Many investors have found this approach most practical. By *averaging* in this manner, their additional investment risk is fixed. If the stock recovers during the time period, either partially or in full, they can end up either with a profit or their loss reduced. Many sophisticated investors would rather average down through calls than any other way. Brokers who approach them and show them this method can often get large accounts.

Frequently, a stockholder is resigned to the possibility of selling out a depreciated stock and accepting his loss. He intends to use whatever money he can salvage from the sale to invest elsewhere. At the same time, the investor is fearful. If he sells the stock originally purchased at $40, which is now selling in the market at $20, he incurs a substantial loss. If he reinvests the proceeds in another stock at $20, he might find himself in a disheartening position . . . his old stock might recover in price and his new stock might go lower!

How can an intelligent registered representative handle this situation? The answer, obviously, is through the use of a call option. A client may buy a call option on the stock that has declined from $40 to $20. After thirty-plus days have elapsed, he can then sell out his stock position. His loss becomes a tax-deductible item. Through his call option, his *interest in his old stock is retained.* At the same time, *he has available the proceeds of the stock sold* to reinvest in the new situation. This way, should his old stock regain its former value, he *still participates in the advance* through his ownership of the call option. If the new stock also goes up, then he becomes a doubly happy investor! If the old stock continues its decline, the investor has only an additional few hundred dollars (the cost of his call) at risk, because the bulk of his money is invested in the new situation.

Leverage

Not the least of the advantages in buying call options, of course, is leverage. The fact that one can control a large amount of stock with a relatively small amount of money is a most attractive feature. Many times, a person with five or ten thousand dollars of risk capital to invest would rather purchase calls on his chosen situation than actually buy the stock. Assume that an investor is intrigued with the capital-gain possibilities in a stock selling in the marketplace at $20 per share. With $5,000 of risk capital, this investor could buy *250 shares,* using his capital to make payment in full; *or,* he could purchase approximately *375 shares* on margin. Still another more dramatic alternative would be to purchase six-month, ten-day call options for about $300 each. This transaction would allow the investor to *control 1600 shares* for the time period involved! Such a maneuver is attractive to many speculators, and it certainly has many valid applications.

In the course of presenting call-option opportunities to prospects and clients, registered representatives must always be mindful of the *suitability* of such purchases for the investor. Rule 405 must constantly be in the back of every broker's mind to serve as a guideline for him to follow.

6 OTC Option Quotes

Broker and investor alike must understand that quotes for OTC options are just that—*quotes*. These quotes are generally not firm [1] prices at which options can be bought. Most New York Stock Exchange, Inc. member firms give these option quotes to prospective buyers in the following way: A quote request is received by the option desk. Usually three option dealers (minimum) are contacted and asked to give their estimates as to what they *believe* it will take for the buyer to purchase a particular option. After obtaining the minimum of three quotes, the option desk will generally inform the broker that the option can be bought somewhere *near* the middle range of the quotes. If the client then decides to purchase the option, the firm's option trader goes to the *lowest quoter* in an attempt to buy the option at the lowest possible price for the client. If the trader is unsuccessful (after a period of approximately thirty minutes to one hour), he will give the order to the middle quoter. This process is repeated until the option trader has exhausted every possibility of buying the option at the quoted price. If a large firm with many branch offices is handling the buy order, all offices are usually notified that an opportunity is available for an option writer to receive a premium. The full details as to time period, name of stock, and premium dollars are listed in the wire.

If the option desk trader can't obtain an execution, he will probably alert the broker to inform his client that it will take *more money* than the original quote to buy the option. The OTC option market is a *negotiated market* rather than an auction market. Many times, it takes several hours—and often an entire day—to complete an OTC option trade. Archaic! Certainly not what investors desire, but that's the way the OTC option market is today.

Changes *are* going on in the option industry, but clients and brokers alike *must know* that buying OTC options is *not like buying stocks*. Quite often, executions simply *cannot be obtained*. Many times, a client wants an OTC option, and even though a market order is given on the premium and a market order on the price of the

---

[1] Some option dealers will make firm quotes, but the premiums they ask are generally so large that they almost preclude a buyer's accepting.

stock, a writer for that contract *has to be located, contacted,* and *encouraged* to write that contract. This process can be time-consuming, especially on lesser-known or volatile stocks.

One other fact that registered representatives should know and relate to clients is that New York taxes OTC call option purchases (but not puts). This tax-rate schedule for OTC call options is: $5 on stocks selling above $20 per share; $3.75 on stocks selling from $10 to $20 per share; and $2.50 on stocks under $10 per share.

7 OTC Put Options: Buying Strategies and Uses

Every registered representative who enters the security selling field and remains in it for any length of time is going to experience bear markets. These down-markets wreak havoc with customers' and brokers' emotions alike. Most brokerage house advice is oriented to the buy side of the market that seeks large potential profits from long positions. Most investors are stock owners, and when down-markets occur, their trading activities slow down or come entirely to a halt.

What can a broker do to help clients and prospects during these inevitable market down-drafts? Does he just sit and watch security situations erode? Does he just offer prayers to the Almighty? Or, does he show clients and prospects where they might possibly find opportunities for profits in depressed markets?

The broker who has studied margin and mastered the strategies available through the purchasing of OTC put option contracts can continue to attract clients. He can help them *seek profits in declining stocks* and can aid them in surviving bear markets. Investors can be very easily oriented to buying OTC puts—perhaps even to the point of looking forward happily to market declines.

OTC put options, however, constitute a *very small percentage of total option purchases.* This is due, in part, to the heavy volume of buy recommendations put out by advisory services and brokerage house research departments. These recommendations focus investors' attention on long positions or toward call options. The American investor's normal, optimistic outlook tends to focus his attention on the up-side possibilities of common stock investments.

However, the knowledgeable registered representative will strive to fill this void concerning the use of OTC put options. He will learn their advantages and their disadvantages. He will make every effort to use them to *protect profits for clients, to seek large capital gains, and for short-term trading purposes.*

For many reasons, few people sell short in the stock market. One of the prime reasons for *not selling short to seek profits* is the adamant stand taken by the Internal Revenue Service on the taxing of regular short sale profits. Their rules call for all *regular short sale* profits to be taxed as *short-term capital gains.* If an investor correctly makes a judgment about a coming stock price decline, and backs up his judgment by properly executing a short sale, and later closes that short sale by purchasing the stock, any profit earned is *taxed as a short-term capital gain.* This is true even if the investor remains short for more than six months before covering his short position. This rule thus deters most investors in high tax brackets from seeking short sale profits in declining markets. It also serves to reduce market liquidity.

Of course, the typical worries associated with the short sale also bother short sellers. These clients are often plagued by an uneasy feeling at having sold a stock they do not own, a stock, furthermore, that has to be replaced in the future at an unknown price. Pity the poor short seller who goes to bed at night only to toss and turn, bothered by thoughts that the company whose shares he is short may suddenly announce a good earnings report, or make public that an acquisition is in the wind, or divulge that a new product is being introduced that could have a substantial impact on sales. Any of these occurrences could force the stock higher. Most short sellers worry and brood over their positions and, quite often, *tend to cover their short positions with either small profits or large losses.*

A practical way exists to simulate a short position in the stock market without the worry associated with being short. This method also provides an absolute guarantee of a fixed, predetermined, dollar risk. At the same time, it provides the opportunity to earn substantial profits—profits earned from a stock price decline that might qualify for the long-term capital-gains tax treatment.

In addition to the emotional factors that accompany a short sale, the short seller also gets into certain mechanical problems. He has to worry about a possible short squeeze. He has to worry about executing the order only on an uptick. Both the fears and the procedural problems are well known and hard to handle for investors as well as the registered representative.

Stock traders are so committed to the long side of the market that they usually overstay losses and generally tend to get out late in a declining stock market. Once out, with substantial capital erosion, they become *less aggressive* and more oriented to simply thinking and talking about the market. The eroded capital, moreover, is usually confined to fixed income, low-, or no-risk investments.

All the foregoing problems (both emotional and mechanical), can often be readily solved by the put contract. Simply defined, a put option gives the holder the right to sell 100 shares of stock at a fixed price for a specified period of time (subject to certain adjustments as per the terms of the contract). The holder is placed in the position of being able to seek profits from stock price declines.

Put options tend to eliminate the *whipsaw* that defeats many would-be short sellers. The whipsaw is created when an investor who sells a stock short encounters a temporary price rise that creates fear of a further price rise. This dread often causes the speculator to cover the short sale at a loss. Later, the initial judgment proves right, and a subsequent decline occurs in the price of the stock.

Ownership of a put option, however, *insulates an investor from adverse price moves.* He does not worry, for he knows he has the right to sell (put) the stock at this fixed price for a period of time. Any interim upward price moves really can't harm him or force him out of his position. He has *full control of the situation, so he doesn't make emotional decisions.*

Should the stock upon which he has purchased a put move down substantially in price, he can *sell* the put option for the value of the contract. Any profits earned on a put contract held and sold after a six-month holding period will be taxed as a *long-term capital gain!* This tax treatment is very different from that of a short seller who cashes a profit after being short over six months. Put options can help to create satisfied clients. As a result, purchasing puts for clients can enable a knowledgeable registered representative to participate happily in down markets.

Put options also can be traded against, like call options. Let's examine how trading against a put is done and how investors can earn profits from this strategy. Assume that a put option is purchased on XYZ at a strike price of 40. Let's also assume that the put option is for a time period of six months and ten days. Should stock XYZ decline in price to 30 within the life of the option, the owner of the put may *fearlessly, risklessly,* enter the market and purchase 100 shares of the stock at 30. "Risklessly," because he owns the right to put (sell) this 100 shares of stock at 40 *any time* within the remaining life of the contract. If he originally paid $600 for his put privilege and he now buys stock at 30, he has locked in for himself *full recovery* of his premium cost, *all related commission expenses, and a substantial profit,* as well.

If, after buying the stock at 30, it rallies in price back to the 40 level within the life of the put, he can sell out the 100-share long position at the $40 price. This course would produce a gain of $1,000. Of course, the investor would have the expense of a commission on the purchase at 30 and the sale at 40. He would also *still be the owner* of his put. The put was intact, *unexercised!* In this situation, the put functions as insurance for making a *riskless* stock market transaction. If, after collecting the gain, the stock should again drop from 40 back down to 35, or even lower, the speculator can enter the market again and buy the stock, hoping for another rally. Should the stock rally up again, he can sell out again. There is *no limit* to how many of these trades can be made within a given period of time against a particular put option. The risk, of course, is *never more* than the cost of the put, and the profit potential can be substantial.

As in the case of a call option, there are two main ways to try to seek stock market profits from puts. One is to go for the large gain by simply buying the put, then holding it to the end of the expiration period. If a stock price drop has occurred at expiration, the put can be sold or exercised and, depending on the size of the decline, a profit obtained, or the premium recovered in part or whole. Should a substantial price fall occur before expiration, the put can be sold or exercised to take advantage of the price drop.

The other method, of course, is to play the down fluctuations of the stock and try to make many numerous short-term capital gains by making purchases of the stock on drops, then selling the stock out on rallies. All of this is done under the protective umbrella of the put.

There is a good caveat for the registered representative to know when he advises clients about these so-called riskless trades against a put option: *Do not recommend closing out at a loss any stock purchases that are protected by a put! Always* close the protected stock purchase with a sale *above* the purchase price. Following this rule accomplishes two important objectives: (1) Every trade against the put will show a gross profit for the client; and (2) compliance problems that might arise if an actively traded account were to show consistent losses will generally be prevented. This method of trading against the put option can be done if the client is *properly educated before* his put purchase.

Sometimes a broker or client tries to become a market "guesser." After buying 100 shares of a stock that has declined below the put price, the broker or client is suddenly smitten with the belief that the stock will decline further. The client is then tempted to sell out the recently purchased stock at a *loss*. This fear opens the client up to the whipsaw reaction, which can be dangerous—it can lose clients as well as their money.

The practice of covering protected trades at a loss should be avoided. If the initial stock purchase made with protection of the put is wrong, and the stock keeps going on down, adhere to this rule: *Exercise the put*. Regain the premium, or whatever part of it is salvageable, and leave it at that. The client can't risk much in this situation and has a great opportunity to profit should the stock fluctuations be in his favor.

A put, in reality, is a *great substitute* for selling stocks short. Unless puts are unobtainable at reasonable prices, there is *little reason for investors to sell stocks short,* (short-against-the-box sales and shorts against calls *excluded*). Many penurious stock traders, however, hate to bear the premium expenses of puts. They prefer to sell short unprotected, except possibly by an actual or mental buy-stop point. *Unhedged short sales* made just to avoid the expense of a put premium are a *poor line of attack*. The best that can be hoped for in a regular short sale is a short-term gain. With a put, at least the opportunity exists to earn a long-term capital gain (if the put is for over six months), as does the possibility of earning substantial trading profits against the put.

Put options certainly appear to be *substantially superior to the buy-stop orders* that many short sellers use. Investors who employ buy-stop orders seem to think that when they sell short stock, they have protected themselves by placing an order to buy the stock at a predetermined level above the short sale price. Many times, however, the buy-stop order is triggered by a market rally or a good announcement, and the short sales are bought in with the execution of the buy-stop order.

Frequently, as much money is lost as would have been spent for the purchase of a put option. In addition to the loss incurred through the triggering of the buy-stop order, the short-selling investor no longer has a position in the stock. Should a subsequent decline occur after the execution of the buy-stop order, the investor *will not participate in that profit situation*.

Another argument that makes a put option seem superior to a short position protected by a buy-stop is that many times, the New York Stock Exchange *bans buy-stop orders*. Also, buy-stop orders frequently get executed away from the buy-stop price. The stop order can provide *no guarantee of execution at the specified price*.

Put options, like call options, can be paid for in a margin account, or even in a cash account, under new Federal Reserve Board rules. Most New York Stock Exchange firms require individuals to buy puts in a general margin account. This payment can be made by cash or check deposited with the broker. Payment for puts can also be made with free credit balances in the client's account, or from the loan value of stocks or other securities on deposit.

How many investors throughout stock market history have been in the position of having wisely bought stock at $10, held it through a rise to the $50 level, and then having to worry over whether they should sell and pay the tax, or hold for future profits? Thousands, perhaps millions, of investors have been faced with this situation and many, many times have made the *wrong decision*. Investors find quite often that if they *don't* sell, the stock declines. The paper profit is wholly or partially dissipated, and maybe even a loss is incurred. Some investors do sell, only to watch the stock reach higher and higher levels. This leaves them frustrated, aggravated, and unhappy *from profits missed*.

The put option can readily solve this dilemma! Assume that an investor buys 100 shares of stock at $10. He holds it over six months, and now finds that the shares are selling in the market at $50. The investor is hesitant to take profits for fear of missing out on a future price rise. He also worries about a possible decline if he stays in the position. For the best of both worlds—*a participation in a future price rise* and *protection against a price drop*—the recommended strategy is to buy a put option.

Our investor may have to pay $650 for a six-month, ten-day put at the $50 level. With the put purchase, he has obtained real peace of mind! Should the stock fall, maybe to the $10 or $20 level, within his time period, he simply exercises his right to put (sell) at the $50 price. He has *preserved his profit* through the expense of a premium. Should the stock rise in price from $50 to $80 or even $100, he will lose the money he spent for his put premium. However, he can gleefully, joyfully, sell his stock out at the higher market price. In addition, the loss of the cost of this put-option premium will be deductible as a capital loss.

The best time-period value for one's money in the OTC put-option world is generally the six-month, ten-day put. There's normally a large supply available from writers. The premium cost is generally not too exorbitant when compared to that asked for shorter time periods. If the put becomes profitable, it can be sold after a holding period of over six months and a long-term capital gain obtained. In addition, the six-month, ten-day put lends itself to the possibility of earning trading profits from market fluctuations that may occur during its life.

Put options are generally cheaper to buy than call options. Some sophisticated people use put options to *insure initial positions.* A put option *bought* at the time of an initial stock purchase and *labeled as insurance* for that purchase gives *complete protection* to the position for the life of the put. This also permits the stock buyer to enjoy an *unlimited* up-side potential in the stock for the duration of the put. The down-side risk in owning the stock is limited to the amount paid as a premium for the put. This provides a *worry-free way* to trade in volatile stocks in *any market climate.*

Put options, their uses and applications, give the knowledgeable registered representative a way to seek profits for clients in market down-drafts or stock price declines. Put options offer a way for clients to protect profits. Put options can be used by clients to shelter initial positions in volatile stocks. Put options are a viable alternative to short sales and the worries and problems associated with short sales. All in all, they are a useful tool for the cautious investor.

Put Options: Problems and Advantages

Acquiring put options can, many times, be difficult. Sometimes, *writers just cannot be found* to issue contracts. This is especially true on very volatile or little-known stocks. Sometimes, a *long delay* takes place while trying to locate a writer for the put. During this lag, the stock may decline substantially, thereby making the put less attractive.

Puts on *high P/E, high quality* growth stocks are usually available at *very low prices* in relation to the dollar amount of stock controlled. These inexpensive puts can work out quite profitably on even relatively minor market dips.

When put losses do occur, they're fully deductible as capital losses. The intelligent broker who has educated clients and prospects to the uses and advantages of put options soon finds that bear markets hold no fear. An income stream is maintained for the broker, while his clients have their capital protected or are earning profits. Can you imagine a broker being cheerful, being happy, or being able even to survive in down-markets?

Many brokers who did not learn the uses of this wonderful tool left the security business in the terrible markets of '62, '66, '69, '70, and '73. They were long position holders only, and they made many trade suggestions that resulted in losses that eventually burnt out their clients and themselves. A good broker must use every product available to develop business and maintain a positive stance toward the stock market. The put option should be a more often used vehicle to arrive at this goal.

8 Straddle Buying Strategy

In the registered representative's constant search for methods to help clients and prospects in their quest for profits, he repeatedly has to face the fact and fear of bear markets. Bear markets, in major or minor force, occur frequently and are of varying durations. During these times of depressed stock prices, investors' confidence is so badly shaken that many refuse to make security purchases. They get disgusted with the securities they have already purchased, and sometimes they abandon the hope of ever making profits.

This inactivity, of course, depresses not only the broker's income; it depresses his attitude, as well. He tends to be less aggressive in his recommendations as well as in his search for new clients and prospects. What should the registered representative do? How can he continue, as a broker, to produce commission income, to seek profit possibilities for clients in these very trying times? *One positive action* that he can take is to *master the buying techniques and uses of straddle options.*

Many brokers have found, to their dismay, that they sometimes encourage clients to buy call options or put options individually, only to find that such calls and puts fail to work out beneficially during the contract life. Then, the client has a loss, the broker earns no commission from stock purchases or sales related to the option contracts, and both client and broker are unhappy. Earlier chapters discussed how calls and puts could be traded against to seek profits. But suppose an investor buys a call and the stock doesn't go up to a level where a riskless short sale can be made against it? In that case, the entire call premium can be lost if the call is not exercised or traded against. No commissions are created by the client's trading in the underlying stock. His risk has been held in check and a tax deduction obtained, but, no profits have been made on the call.

Suppose a client has been influenced to buy a put and the stock does not decline so that the put will be valuable. Suppose that no "riskless" stock purchases can be made fully insured by the put. If that situation occurs, the client loses his put premium, partially or wholly, and the broker earns no stock commissions.

The *straddle option can provide workable solutions* in the

foregoing situations. The broker who has acquired straddle knowledge can continue to help clients in *any type of market*. The straddle is probably the greatest device ever for attacking the search for stock market profits in volatile issues on a continuing basis.

The straddle is a combination of options. Briefly defined, a straddle is a put on 100 shares of stock *and* a call on 100 shares of stock at the *same striking price* for the *same period of time*. A straddle holder has two rights. If he uses one, he does not obviate or invalidate the other. The straddle buyer should take the attitude that *no one really knows the future price of any stock*. Nobody can really know what will happen to the price in the next short period of time to current volatile issues such as Fairchild Camera, Itek, Natomas, and Syntex. What professional straddle buyers *do* know is that these are *volatile, high P/E, very high risk* situations that can go up suddenly or down suddenly. In the professional straddle buyer's eyes, these stocks are sure . . . to fluctuate.

People who buy straddles in their search for stock market profits generally differ from those who buy individual puts and individual calls. The straddle buyer doesn't want to be forced to guess the market direction of a particular stock in a given time period. This is what call buyers and put buyers *must do* when they choose their time and their particular call or put option.

The straddle buyer just wants a fluctuation in the price of the stock to occur, and he couldn't care less whether this fluctuation is up or down. His belief is that if he buys a straddle on a volatile stock and the stock moves *substantially up,* he may recover the entire premium cost of the straddle, the stock commission expense involved, and a profit . . . all from exercising, selling, or trading against the call part of the straddle. Should the stock move *down substantially,* he has the opportunity to recover his premium cost, the stock commission cost, and a profit from exercising, selling, or trading against the put part of the straddle.

A significant feature to the straddle buyer is that his risk of *losing his straddle premium in its entirety,* in his opinion, is *very, very little*—perhaps almost nil due to the fluctuating nature of volatile stocks. It is true that he may *lose part* of his straddle premium from an *insufficient price movement* in either direction. It is also true that a greater premium is required than for the purchase of a put or call. But, all in all, the risk of loss of premium dollars appears to be *much, much less* than that of the single option buyer.

A registered representative can develop a substantial business by explaining straddle-buying concepts to clients and prospects. Straddles are especially attractive to those who would love to trade in the stock market but fear to do so because of the large risks that normally go with volatile stocks. Many investors are frequently tempted to sell stocks short. They relish the idea of buying high P/E stocks but the *fear of large losses* keeps them from doing so.

The challenge of the market is exciting to broker and customer alike; yet, many of those who experienced the '69–'70 and '73 disaster markets were so damaged that their enthusiasm—their desire to challenge the stock market with their judgment—was dimmed substantially. Many investors during those terrible times had big percentage losses in the market. Certainly their enjoyment of the stock market disappeared.

A knowledgeable stock broker who presents the *straddle strategy* to these investors can rekindle their enthusiasm for the market. Straddle strategy offers the investor an absolutely predetermined risk—his straddle premium. At the same time, he gets a *relatively unlimited profit* potential. In order to profit, he *no longer has to be right on the market direction*. What a wonderful set of facts to present to clients and prospects! A quite different way to present stock market challenges and opportunities to potential investors! Straddle owners just have to have movement, either up or down, to earn profits from straddles.

Let's see how these potential profits can be earned by an investor. There are really three ways to pursue profit through the purchase of straddles. The first method is simply to buy a straddle on a volatile stock. Hold the straddle until it expires, and then sell off whichever part of the straddle—the put or the call—is profitable at that time. The investor in this situation is hoping for a sufficiently large move up or down in the price of the stock to regain the cost of the straddle, the stock commission costs, and a profit. This method doesn't require any particular ability on the part of the investor or the broker. All that is involved is buying the straddle and holding it in position until a large move has occurred. (This, of course, can happen before the expiration of the straddle.) The risk of losing the entire straddle premium is small, as we pointed out earlier, due to the volatile nature of stocks. It seldom happens that a volatile stock stays at the same level for any given period of time.

The second way to seek profits through a straddle purchase is to buy the straddle on a volatile issue and attempt to earn short-term trading profits in the stock market while using the *straddle as an insurance policy* to limit the risk.

Assume the following facts. An investor purchases a 95-day

straddle on XYZ at 40. He pays a premium of $800 for the straddle. In the first 30 days, the stock price moves from 40 to 50. At this point, the broker can suggest to the client (the client, if properly attuned to straddle strategy, may take the initiative himself), to sell 100 shares of XYZ short at 50. The client will have to deposit the necessary collateral requirement for the short sale.

At this point, the investor is in a riskless position. He owns a straddle with the strike price fixed at 40. He has sold short 100 shares at 50. What can happen to this stock at 50? It could go up, or it could go down. No one has the power to foresee in which direction the price will go. Should it decline from $50 back to the level of $40 before the expiration of the straddle, the investor simply buys 100 shares of the stock in the open market to close out the short sale. This would earn him a $1,000 gross profit, reduced by the applicable commission expenses. He *still owns* the straddle.

After closing out the profitable short sale at $40, the stock can take one of two courses. It could go up, or it could go down. Should it again advance in price above $40, the straddle holder can again *short the stock risklessly,* knowing that the call part of the straddle can be exercised any time, giving full protection for the short sale. Should the stock, however, decline from the $40 level to $30, he can buy 100 shares at $30, knowing that he can exercise his right to put (sell) 100 shares at $40 any time during the life of the straddle. Again, the investor is making an insured, riskless trade in the stock market. Should the stock rally back to the $40 price, after buying it at $30, he can sell the stock and earn for himself $1,000 gross profit, reduced by the applicable commissions. His ownership of the straddle is still intact.

The investor who employs the foregoing strategy is simply using a straddle as insurance to make protected short sales or long purchases in the stock market *only after a market move away from the straddle strike price* has occurred. Many times, thousands of dollars of profits can be earned on a *premium risk* of only hundreds of dollars.

Please note that the risk of a volatile stock's not moving up or down is little; the investor might lose part of his straddle premium, but seldom all of it. Often, he may make enough successful trades against the straddle to earn a very handsome return on his capital.

The straddle buyer normally *hopes to make many profits* on either or both sides of the straddle option through stock trades, long or short, within the life of the option. This concept can attract many prospects to the stock market. It can create prospects from people who would not normally be interested because of the presumed risk that exists in trading volatile issues. Informed registered representatives should point out to prospects and clients the fun and exhilaration of straddle trading, as well as the profit potential.

Also note that successful trading against the straddle creates short-term capital gains. In recent years, many investors have been left holding carry-forward, long-term capital losses and short-term capital losses. To these investors, *any type of gain* is highly attractive and fully applicable against capital losses in any form.

The third method for seeking profits through straddle purchases is one that is used by many sophisticated, professional straddle traders. Use the figures from our previous example: striking price, $40; time period, 95 days; premium cost, $800. On a price move to $50, the straddle holder *exercises his right to call* for the stock at $40. He then sells out the stock at $50, cashing in a $1,000 gain, reduced by commissions. Under new New York Stock Exchange rules, he *does not need any additional capital* to call for (buy) the stock and sell it if he does both on the same day. This strategy involves exercising the call (or put) and selling (or buying) the stock at the first opportunity within the straddle life when all his premium risk and expenses can be regained.

Suppose the stock moves a week or a month into the life of the straddle. In this case, upon exercising one straddle part, he still owns the remaining part of the straddle (the put, in our example) as a *free option*. Should the stock subsequently decline within the life of the straddle, the put could become valuable. In the meantime, he has recovered all his premium cost and commission expense, and *made a profit* on the transaction from the call portion of the straddle.

With the proceeds from the exercised call, the investor then buys a new straddle, on the same stock or a different volatile stock. Assume that the proceeds are used to buy a straddle on the same stock at the $40 level. If the stock declines from $40 to $30 in the first thirty or sixty days in the life of the new straddle, the investor can exercise his right to put the stock at $40 after buying 100 shares in the open market at $30. By so doing, he earns a $1,000 profit, less the commissions. This leaves him with a free call option at $40. The proceeds from exercising the put are now available for reinvestment in still another straddle.

This practice can be highly attractive to investors, because *no additional capital is necessary* to obtain the profits in the stock. *You may buy and sell stock the same day, as long as you are calling or putting,* and *put up no capital to do so.*

In an earlier example, the investor had to deposit sufficient collateral with a broker to trade against the straddle. Cash or securities were needed to margin the short sale or long purchase of the stock. In this example, when you are exercising a call or put and liquidating the stock, you do not have to put up any money to make these trades. This is a *little-known, highly attractive feature* of puts and calls.

Registered representatives dealing in options soon learn that every time they buy a straddle for a client, they will generally earn at least two round-lot commissions. The investor who owns a straddle will either buy the stock and sell it out through the exercise of his put, or sell the stock and buy the stock through the exercise of the call. Also, he may trade against the straddle many times during its lifetime. The RR can expect a minimum of two round-lot commissions from the purchase of every straddle.

There are several general guidelines for advising clients about the purchase of straddles.

1. Suggest to the investor that he limit his straddle premium expense to not over *20%* of the current market price for a *95-day straddle option*.

2. Try to suggest the purchase of straddle options in a cost range of 15 to 18% of the current market price. The premiums are negotiable.

3. Buy straddles *only on volatile stocks* or stocks you believe, for whatever reason, might become volatile within the near future.

4. Most straddle buyers (other than option dealers) avoid buying straddles for thirty-five days and sixty-five days since extremely short time periods generally do not give enough time for the desired price movements to occur. The trading opportunities generally become more limited. The most popular straddle life is usually ninety-five days.

5. There is generally a great supply of 95-day straddles available because this time period is attractive to option writers, too.

6. Usually, it is not advisable to buy straddles on stocks under $20 because of the relatively low profit potential from the put option.

7. The most popular striking price for straddles ranges from $40 to $60.

8. Straddles on marginable, over-the-counter stocks are much harder to come by and usually much greater in cost.

Six-month, ten-day straddles are not purchased as often as ninety-five day straddles by professional straddle buyers, simply because they cost more. In addition, the standard practice of cutting short the profit potential by trading against or exercising part of a straddle turns knowledgeable investors away from these longer-lifetime straddles. Professional straddle buyers generally are not out to make a really large gain in one particular direction, except for the one case pointed out earlier. The usual intent *is to earn quick, continual, short-term profits* in all types of markets.

Put and call dealers who inventory straddles for resale at a mark-up will often buy thirty-five and sixty-five day straddles in order to reduce the risk to their capital. Of course, they must have the sales ability to market straddles as "specials," in part or whole.

Straddle-trading, from the broker's point of view, is perhaps the best single way to develop trading accounts—trading accounts that can last and have the *opportunity to do well in any type of market*; trading accounts that have complete knowledge of and *limits on their risk capital;* trading accounts that retain *relatively unlimited profit potential.*

9 Option Writing

Almost all registered representatives hope to acquire large accounts of wealthy investors. They hope that if they get these accounts, they will reap a great, steady harvest of commissions.

Newly registered brokers are often successful in opening accounts for investors with substantial assets. However, these registered representatives sometimes discover that such accounts produce *fewer* commission dollars per year than actively traded accounts with only $10,000 to $25,000 in assets! This discovery can be a rude awakening for the broker.

Many large security portfolios ($100,000 to $1 million or more) *have low cost basis* securities. The owners of these securities are very reluctant to dispose of them because they will incur capital-gains tax. Substantial accounts of this nature purchase or sell shares only occasionally. Frequently, large accounts have had the benefit of money management techniques, perhaps from investment advisors, perhaps from a diligent portfolio owner's constant attention. The assets may have been prudently invested to include municipal bonds, corporate bonds, quality growth stocks, and quality income stocks. After giving thought to possible tax consequences, quite often it is found that very few changes need to be made.

The registered representative often finds that these accounts have placed all or part of their assets with money managers such as bank trust departments, mutual funds (either load or no-load), or investment advisors. In many cases, the commission throwoff from these managed assets is very small. Sometimes, in fact, commissions are completely unavailable for the registered representative who has an account for an individual, the bulk of whose funds are professionally controlled. In such a case, the broker may have opened an account via a small trade on a new issue, a syndicate item, or a municipal bond purchase. The client may even ask the investment advisor to place business through the registered representative, but quite often, this request cannot be fulfilled.

What can a registered representative do to encourage investors with high-value portfolios to use his services as a broker? What can he do for an investor that might enhance the profit potential of the investor's assets? One answer is to *learn option-writing techniques!*

Option writing can frequently be the key to unlocking the assets of a substantial investor. Knowledgeable, forward-thinking registered representatives should try to learn everything possible about writing options. Their study should be deep and thorough, so that the tax implications are mastered as well as the risk reduction and profit potential in issuing option contracts.

Once he has learned option writing strategy, the registered representative must learn how to convey this information to clients and prospects. He must properly sell suitable investors on the benefits of option writing to their particular investment program.

Many times, investors with substantial assets who have been devotees of outside money management will become fascinated and intrigued by the possibilities and opportunities presented in option writing. Frequently, these individuals will retrieve their assets, or a large portion of them, from their money managers and utilize the retrieved funds in an option writing program. However, this can only occur after option writing has been *properly explained* to a prospect by a well-informed registered representative.

Why would a substantial investor want to enter option writing activities? Why would he choose to retrieve monies under management to place in an option writing program? These are fair questions.

Let's examine the basics involved in option writing before we get into specifics. People of substantial wealth who place their money with money managers do so to avoid investment decision making and record keeping. They generally expect to obtain three "prudent man" principles of investing through the expertise of the money manager.

Dollar Cost Averaging

This is a money management technique that involves the investing of funds at periodic intervals over a period of time. The thought behind this concept is that no one is ever certain that the current market is high or low. By flowing the money into investments in relatively equal amounts over a time frame, it is believed that a better result may be obtained. It is considered to be a risk-reducing technique.

Diversification

By investing money in many different securities, the risk is so spread that no single bad judgment will greatly affect the overall portfolio. *In return for the risk reduction, diversification generally serves to limit profit potential.*

Selectivity

Money managers' selections of security investments *should be superior* to those of most nonexperts, since they give full time to managing investments. The money manager's educational background and access to current investment information should result in superior timing of investment decisions.

Many wealthy investors have found out that placing money under management—whether with an investment advisor, a mutual fund, or a bank trust department—*does not guarantee a profit* or any specific return on their investment.

Many times—especially in 1969–70 and 1973—money managers have done poorly with assets entrusted to them. Even in good financial markets, many of them have averaged a return equal only to that of money in a bank savings account or in high quality bonds. Some investment advisors and money managers have done better than to barely outperform bond or savings bank interest, but many have not. Furthermore, the assets under their fee management are always exposed to a *greater risk* than in the bank or in bonds.

Substantial investors everywhere are frighteningly aware that the relief from decision-making responsibility and the avoidance of record keeping by giving someone else discretionary powers over their money *often doesn't produce the results they want.* It is this type of investor who is most open and most inclined to listen to a learned registered representative explain how the investor can participate in option-writing activities.

Option writing offers the asset-laden investor who is a decision maker the opportunity to apply all the prudent man principles of investing—dollar cost averaging, diversification, and expert selection. (The selections can be his own, or the research recommendations of the firm where the account is lodged, or from any source in which he has confidence.) In addition to being decisive, an option writer must have an interest in, and an understanding of, the stock market. He should also be an accurate recordkeeper.

In addition to these prudent man investing principles, option writing offers something else—something that is *not available* through other money management techniques. It offers premium dollars *paid cash in advance* in return for issuing an option contract. *This prepaid money can amount to hundreds or thousands of dollars for every transaction entered* into by the writer of the option. In other words, option writing offers a *head start* on every hundred shares that go into the portfolio. In the investment world, this is a very unusual and attractive feature.

This prepaid "profit" is the option premium paid to the writer for assuming the risk in the underlying stock. The stock must, within the time period of the option, move against the writer for him to lose the premium or incur a loss. Through this medium, an investor does have actual dollars in advance that represent a potential profit.

This is different from almost all forms of investing in securities. *With most security investments, the buyer starts out at a loss!* He is usually out the commission or markup to buy the security—be it stock, or bonds, or a load mutual fund. He is also out the spread between bid and ask that exists in stock and bond markets. With load mutual funds, stocks, and bonds that are not intended to be held to maturity, he has to hope for a future price rise in the security or bond to overcome the commission and the spread between bid and ask, and to return him a profit.

The investor who takes part in option writing has the prepaid premium *in his pocket* the *very next day* after writing the option contract. This money-in-advance feature can be a great tool for the success-oriented broker to use in obtaining option-writing accounts.

Most option writers are percentage-minded people with substantial capital. They hope to earn possibly 15 to 20 percent annual return on their capital committed to option writing. Of course, no guarantee exists that they will earn 15 to 20 percent. This is simply a goal—a calculated expectation they have, and that many achieve.

Option writers generally conduct their activities from their homes or make use of brokerage office facilities. Option writing as a business activity generally *avoids* the expenses of rent, utilities, and employees. Very large, institutional-type option writers do, however, incur these expenses in addition to commission expenses.

Option issuers do have the advantage of prepaid premiums. They hope to retain and bring down to net a large part of these premiums during the course of their option-writing activities. Option writers can write many different kinds of option contracts. They can be either bullish option writers or bearish option writers, as well as hedge option writers.

During these next chapters, we will examine the various ways an option writer can go about seeking the fabled 15 to 20 percent a year return on his capital. We will also examine the risks he incurs and the costs he experiences in his search.

The registered representative seeking option-writing business and the development of option-writing prospects will soon learn that option buyers are primarily interested in three main types of contracts—the put, the call, and the straddle. Other combinations (OTC options) of puts and calls, such as spreads, straps, and strips, are rarely dealt in.

In writing puts, calls, and straddles, the writer receives premium dollars that are the *limit on his profit*. He incurs or insures the stock market risk for the buyer of the option in return for the advance payment. These risks can often be substantial. Knowledgeable registered representatives will take great care to learn all the different strategies available to writers of options—strategies that might serve to mitigate and alleviate the writers' assumptions of risk.

Let's look first at the stance of a bullish option writer—his viewpoints, his goals. Let's observe how the bullish option writer approaches the writing of OTC calls, puts, and straddles.

10 Bullish OTC Call Writing

The bullish OTC call-option writer takes the viewpoint (and this, perhaps, is the most popular viewpoint in the option-writing industry, but not necessarily the most correct) that he is willing to be long stock. The bullish OTC call writer takes the viewpoint that the downside risk of his long position is, in his opinion, less dangerous than a short position in the same stock. The bullish OTC call-option writer believes that the premium dollars paid to him for assuming the risk of owning the stock are sufficient compensation in a normal market environment. He is convinced that the advance dollars really offer him the opportunity to earn his goal of 15 to 20 percent annually on his stock commitments.

The bullish OTC call-option writer allocates the amount of capital that he wishes to commit to option writing. He then *plans* an OTC call-option writing program. In planning his program, he should establish a set of criteria that he hopes will guide him to a successful conclusion.

A typical set of criteria for a bullish OTC call writer is as follows:

1. *Write OTC calls mainly on New York Stock Exchange, Inc. stocks.* (Many OTC call option writers restrict their OTC call writing to OTC calls on New York Stock Exchange, Inc. stocks that are rated B or better by Standard & Poor's.)
2. *Issue OTC calls on stocks that are highly rated for year-ahead performance* by a financial service such as Value Line.
3. *Write OTC calls for periods longer than six months.*
4. *Do not issue OTC calls that do not produce at least $200 in advance.*
5. *Do not buy stock to collateralize a six-month, ten-day OTC call,* (even if the stock quality is high), *if the premium is less than 9%* of the current market price.
6. *Write OTC calls on stocks that are well within their normal P/E and historical price range.*
7. *Diversify so that no more than 10% of the option-writing funds are committed to any one stock.*
8. *Space the expiration dates* of option contracts so that dollar cost averaging can be effected.

11 Bullish OTC Put Writing

In the previous chapter, we discussed how a bullish OTC call writer attempts to earn 15 to 20 percent annually on his capital. Bullish OTC call writers normally experience a commission on stock bought to collateralize the call (unless the stock has been purchased on a net basis in a principal transaction). The registered representative benefits from the commission, and with most NYSE member firms, will receive a portion of the endorsement fee that the firm receives from the put and call dealer who negotiated the option contract. The registered representative can also look forward to the expiration date, when another commission will be received if the stock is called away.

When a call option is exercised against the bullish writer, funds become available to reinvest. Profits have been earned by the writer, and commissions by the broker—a thoroughly happy situation for both. A bullish OTC call issuance takes place when the writer *positions the stock* and *takes the risk* that the stock might go down more than the premium received during the time period of the option contract. Bullish OTC call writers are *always faced with the expense of two commissions* should their judgments prove right. One commission is incurred to buy the stock to collateralize the OTC call, and the second commission is incurred when the stock is called (sold), or otherwise disposed of. The commission expense, of course, detracts from the option writer's gross premium income, but it represents the bulk of all expenses incurred by option writers.

Bullish OTC put writing is quite different from bullish OTC call writing. The bullish OTC put writer issues put contracts but incurs *no immediate commission expense*. He *reserves cash* to pay for stock should the put be exercised. He accepts market risk on the down side of the market, as does the bullish OTC call writer. The stock underlying the put contract can drop within the time period, forcing the OTC put writer to be a stock owner through exercise of the put.

The focus of the bullish OTC put issuer is on a stock price rise through the put life. If this rise occurs, the put will *not be exercised,* and at expiration the *entire put premium will be earned* and brought down to net. Please note again that a bullish OTC put writer incurs *no commission expense for every right judgment.*

What a difference between the results from his right judgments as opposed to the results from the bullish OTC call writer's correct judgments! The bullish OTC put writer and bullish OTC call writer *both incur the same risk—that of the stock declining.* One great difference in possible return on capital is that the bullish OTC put writer has the *opportunity* to earn his premium *free of all expenses.* After issuing the put, should the stock rise and stay above the put price, *no exercise* will take place. The put grantor will, therefore, have netted the premium and avoided any stock commission expense.

There are other advantages that also accrue to a bullish OTC put writer, and the knowledgeable registered representative should be aware of them. Presented properly to sophisticated, intelligent investors, substantial business may result. Examine some of these advantages very carefully.

Assume that an option writer owns $100,000 of fully paid for marginable stocks. The loan value on this $100,000 worth of stock is currently 35 percent. The dollar loan amount in this example would equal $35,000. The bullish OTC put writer, therefore, could employ the *loan value leverage* available—there are many large NYSE member firms that permit option writing activities—and issue at least $70,000 of "naked" put options using the loan value of his long position as collateral.

This allows the writer to take in put premiums on $70,000 worth of securities and yet not create a debit balance for himself at all! Seemingly unbelievable, yet true! Additional leverage can be gained by using the premiums received from the sale of puts on the $70,000 worth of stocks to issue still more put contracts.

The registered representative who learns to present this facet may win some really substantial clients for himself. Additional participation in bull markets can be had without creating a debit balance! No interest charges to be paid as there are with a debit balance! An opportunity to earn profits yet *pay no stock commissions* for every right judgment!

Risk is ever-present due to the put liability. If the writer is wrong, he is forced to buy stock at the specified price. Should puts be exercised against a writer, he must be prepared to make decisions . . . decisions as to whether he should immediately sell the put stock, or whether he should inventory it and hope for a recovery in price.

New York Stock Exchange rules governing *minimum margin deposits* for put writers permit a deposit of only 25 percent of the market value of the stock specified in the put contract plus or minus any difference between market price and strike price. There are not (at this time) many NYSE member firms who permit this minimum 25 percent collateralization.

Should a writer be doing business with a firm that permits the minimum, he can write puts on $140,000 worth of stock (loan value on $100,000 = $35,000; 25% deposit on $140,000 of puts = $35,000) and create no debit balance. This leverage can be further increased by utilizing the premiums received to collateralize additional puts.

The sword of leverage has two edges, as we have said. Bullish put writing can prove dangerous if the writer's judgment is wrong and securities begin to decline in value. He is forced to buy stock at prices higher than the current market and has to add additional capital to retain the purchased stock.

As all option writers are, bullish put writers are entitled to use the premium being paid to them to apply against the margin requirement of their naked puts. Most NYSE member firms today require a writer of naked puts or calls to have a minimum amount of equity in his account in addition to the option margin requirement. Usually this equity requirement is from $25,000 to $50,000. Once having met the equity requirement, the writer must collateralize, over and above his equity, the option requirement for the naked contract being issued.

Let's observe closely the leverage available for a bullish put writer meeting the $25,000 minimum equity and writing options with an NYSE member firm that allows him to deposit 25 percent to collateralize a naked put. Assume that a writer issues a one year naked put on volatile stock XYZ at 40 for $1,000. He receives credit for the $1,000 premium the next day. The option requirement to collateralize the put at 40 would be $1,000 (the 25% collateral due in five business days). The premium being collected equals the deposit needed. Therefore, he *needs no additional funds of his own* to make the required deposit! It may seem incredible, but it is absolutely true. The option requirement is met by the premium payment! The writer is attempting to earn, with a correct judgment, $1,000 with *no commission* expense and no other collateral deposit from his own funds or securities!

If the bullish OTC put writer is doing business with a member firm that requires 50 percent of the naked put contract as collateral, he has to deposit $1,000 of his own funds for issuance of the put at

40. This amount is in addition to the $1,000 being received as the put premium. The writer is depositing $1,000 in an attempt to earn $1,000 (and at the same time avoid commission expense) should his judgment prove right. In our example, writing a long-term naked put on a stock is a unique way to try to double one's money. This market method attracts many substantial investors. Not the least of the attractions is the risk cushion the put premium provides.

Before a registered representative becomes all enthused over the concept of writing naked puts against a cash reserve, he should be aware of the *disadvantage* that occrues to *successful bullish put writers*. The disadvantage is that the Internal Revenue Service *taxes expired premium income* (unless the expired premiums are lapsed parts of straddles) as ordinary income in the year of expiration—income that is taxed at the highest bracket of the investor. The bullish put writer, therefore, *can never earn* the benefit of long-term capital gain treatment for his earned premium income.

In approaching potential option writers, registered representatives can also point out that writing puts against cash offers a way for writers to *acquire desired stocks at cheaper prices* than those available in the current market at the time of contract issuance. If the desired stocks are not acquired due to a price rise, the bullish put writer is compensated by an earned premium. The collateral used to back put contracts is often Treasury bills or bonds, so the bullish put writer's funds perform double duty. Interest is earned on the collateral in addition to the premium collected.

If a bullish put writer issues a put and the stock goes down, the put will be exercised. The cost basis for tax purposes is the price at which the put is exercised *reduced by the premium* received. Upon exercise, the writer will then be an owner of stock— stock that he wouldn't have minded owning at the time the put commitment was originally made. Shares owned at a *reduced cost basis!* Should the stock rise, instead, the put premium earned is *free and clear* of all commission expenses. At the expiration of the successfully written put, the capital used to collateralize the put can be used either to write another put or to invest elsewhere.

12 Bullish OTC Straddle Writing

Straddles are combinations of options. One put and one call on 100 shares of stock at the same striking price for the same period of time comprise a straddle. The registered representative in contact with option writers and potential option writers can stress the advantages and strategies involved in writing straddle options as opposed to writing individual calls and puts.

One advantage in writing straddles is the larger premium. Straddle premiums are generally 1.7 times greater than call premiums for the same period of time.

The writer who is bullish enough to buy 200 shares of stock and write two call options makes the risk assumption that the 200 shares of stock will not decline enough during the time period to create a loss for him after taking into account the premiums received. His total possible profit is limited to the premium paid to him. *The potential gain is reduced by commissions paid to buy and sell the 200 shares* should the stock be called away.

The bullish writer might also buy *100* shares of stock and sell a straddle option, taking in the larger premium. If his judgment proves right and the stock rises, the call part of the straddle is exercised. This forces the bullish straddle writer to sell his 100 shares at the specified price. This forced sale can occur any time during the contract life. For his correct judgment, the bullish straddle writer would have incurred a commission on *only 100 shares of stock bought and on only 100 shares called away (sold)*.

If the stock declines and the put is exercised, the writer is forced to purchase the other 100 shares of stock, finding himself the owner of 200 shares. Very rarely are both parts of a straddle exercised against a straddle writer.

There are special tax advantages to straddle writers that the knowledgeable registered representative must learn and make known to potential option writers. These tax advantages often incline an investor toward option writing activities. The Internal Revenue Service has ruled that the writer of a straddle must allocate the premium received for the straddle between the put option and the call option. A uniform allocation is recommended. Normally, 55 percent of a straddle premium is allocated to the call portion of the straddle, and 45 percent of the straddle premium is allocated to the put portion of the straddle. Many writers use a 50/50 allocation. As long as the allocation is *consistent* and *uniform* there should be little objection by the Internal Revenue Service.

Earlier chapters pointed out that one of the disadvantages in writing call options and put options uncombined is the tax treatment upon expiration. If a put option written against cash *expires,* the put premium *becomes ordinary income* to the writer of the option in the year of expiration. Should a call option be written and expire, the premium income is treated as *ordinary income* to the writer of the option in the year of expiration. Expired premium profits can be offset to a limited extent by capital losses that might have been incurred.[1]

Sometimes, a writer realizes capital losses from selling stocks that were originally bought to collateralize option contracts, but despite his loss (beyond $1,000), he has to pay taxes on the *expired premium* income that he receives. This is distasteful. There are many high bracket writers who will not write calls or puts uncombined because of this tax situation. They *like* the tax treatment afforded writers of straddles.

The Internal Revenue Service has determined that if a straddle is issued and one part of the straddle lapses (in other words, if the call is exercised and the put expires or if the put is exercised and the call expires), the lapsed part is treated as a *short-term capital gain*—a gain that can be applied as an offset against any *short- or long-term loss* that exists.

The straddle writer generally experiences *no ordinary income,* unlike the writer of uncombined, expired calls or puts. This tax treatment is favorable and attractive. Option writers also find it easier to write straddles because there is a greater demand for straddles on a greater variety of stocks than there is for individual puts or calls. This demand is greater because option dealers, many times, are willing to position straddles as part of their inventory. This willingness to assume risk serves to broaden the market for options.

Dealers take the capital risk because they believe they have a

---

[1] The Internal Revenue Service does allow up to $1,000 of short-term capital losses to be applied as a deduction against ordinary income. Any short-term losses greater than $1,000 may be carried forward indefinitely until eventually used up.

Long-term capital losses can also be used as a deduction against ordinary income up to the limit of $1,000 in any taxable year. However, it takes $2,000 of long-term losses to gain a $1,000 deduction against ordinary income. Long-term capital losses can also be carried forward indefinitely until used up.

chance to sell one or both parts of the straddle profitably. If they are unable to market the options, the potential still exists for a market move in the stock that will provide the dealer with a chance to regain the straddle premium he paid to the option writer.

If a bullish writer issues a straddle on a stock and the stock does happen to decline, he will be put with the stock. The cost of the stock he must buy is *reduced* by the *portion* of the straddle premium he allocated to the put.

The bullish straddle writer, upon being put, *does not declare as income* the put premium allocated as part of the straddle he granted. The lapsed call premium provides a short-term capital gain for him—a gain that can be used to offset any capital losses sustained or carried forward from previous years.

The investor embarking on straddle writing quickly realizes that every straddle he writes normally involves the expense of two round-lot commissions. One commission is incurred when stock is bought to back the straddle, and another commission is expended when stock is either called away or put to the writer.

A registered representative should alert straddle writers to carefully evaluate the risk in writing straddles. Capital should be reserved to back the put parts of straddles.

Bullish OTC straddle writers normally take extreme care to *know the stocks they buy* to collateralize straddles. Bullish writers should adhere to criteria similar to those listed in the chapter on bullish call writers. Bullish straddle writing, like all option writing, requires of the writer the *ability to be a decision maker*. He has to be able and willing to make a *risk choice*. He must view the straddle premium offered as a *limited profit* that can only be earned *if* he correctly determines the direction of the stock during the particular time period.

Should the bullish straddle writer's judgment prove wrong, he loses on the stock bought to back the straddle, and in addition, he *must bear the loss on another 100 shares* that will be put to him.

Assume that a bullish writer buys 100 shares of ZYX at 40 and issues a 95-day straddle for a premium of $800. If the stock *declines only four points,* the writer has *lost all* the protection afforded by the large 20 percent premium.

13 Bearish OTC Option Writing

A phrase indigenous to the option market and intriguing to most people unacquainted with the option market is the term *naked option*. This term is used to designate a call, put, or straddle issued by an option writer who has *no position in the security* at the time he issues the contract. The writer is naked, uncovered, bare . . . without stock!

The registered representative should be well aware that many naked option writers *seek to earn far more* than the normal 15 to 20 percent annual income that is sought by most conservative, covered, option writers.

Naked OTC call writers are usually the most sophisticated and learned of all option writers. Their accounts are usually very active and require from the registered representative close observance and much service.

Naked call writers generally are market bears. They tend to believe the stock direction will be down during the life of their naked call contracts. These writers also believe that *call option buyers as a whole are generally wrong* within their time frame.

Naked call writers also are smitten with the belief that the group of *call option buyers who are wrong most often* are those call buyers who buy calls for short periods of time—35 days, 65 days, 95 days— or anything less than six months. Of these short-term call buyers, the bearish writer believes the buyer who buys calls in small quantities, such as one, two, or three, is usually the *most wrong of all.*

With these premises in mind, the naked call writer attempts to earn premium profits by writing call options on stocks for short time periods. He feels that in so doing, his risk exposure is low. Thirty-five, sixty-five, and ninety-five day contracts are the contracts most frequently issued by naked call writers.

The bearish call writer feels he is dealing with the unsophisticated small investor who is most likely to err. The assumption of the naked call writer is that men and women of substantial wealth who are very smart in the market buy call options *only* when the opportunity exists to earn *long-term capital gains* if their judgments prove correct.

Wealthy investors who enter the option market normally buy large quantities of call options, perhaps 50, 100, or more at a time. Naked OTC call writers try to ferret out the volume demand for call options on a particular stock. A large volume bid may make them wary of issuing the contracts.

The naked call writer is further rewarded for correct judgments by *not having to expend* commissions. This no-commission situation occurs when he chooses not to buy stock when issuing a call. Upon the lapse of the call, he has no commission expense whatever and has earned the call premium in its entirety.

Under present OTC option-writing practice, the bearish writer must have an account with an NYSE member firm that will endorse naked option contracts for him. The firm will generally require some minimum equity in the account, plus naked option margin requirements.

The naked call writer also knows that if his judgment is wrong and the stock rises instead of falls, there are several lines of defense available to him. If the issue is NYSE-listed, one such strategy is to place a buy-stop order to obtain the stock if it goes to a predetermined level above the call-option striking price. The usual practice in this defense is to *place a stop order to buy the stock* at the strike price plus the premium collected. This method usually produces a premium profit on all stocks that decline or stay under the buy-stop order.

The drawback to this buy-stop defense is that a whipsaw might occur. The whipsaw can happen if the stock rises within the time period to a level where the buy-stop order is triggered, thus forcing the writer into a stock purchase. After the purchase, the stock might subsequently decline.

Even this sequence of events would not necessarily create a loss (other than commission expense) unless the stock, after being positioned, declines below the strike price. Some naked call writers place buy-stops closer to the strike than the premium amount. They hope to break even on forced purchases, including commission expenses. However, closer stops increase the chances of a whipsaw's developing. Each writer must determine his own formula for defending naked OTC call positions.

Another defense that is sometimes used by naked OTC call writers is to sell an opposite option. If, upon issuance of a naked call, the stock should rise to a predetermined level, the writer can try to sell a put option at the then higher level. This action provides more protection by taking in another premium, and it still leaves the writer bare of stock for the time being. Upon issuing the put, the possibility then exists of being forced to acquire the stock, should it decline. The naked call writer is additionally protected against a further rise of the stock by the amount of the premium received for the put.

Let's look at an example. A naked call writer issues a call for 95 days on XYZ at 30 for a premium of $300. Thirty days after issuance, the stock rises to 33, and the writer attempts a defense. At the 33 level, he is able to sell a 65-day put for $250. At this point, he has received $550 in premiums ($300 for the call at 30 and $250 for the put at 33), and still has *no stock position!* If the stock declines from 33, the writer will be put. This forced purchase makes stock available to deliver if the call at 30 is exercised. The writer's eventual position is protected by the two premiums he has received.

If the stock is below the 33 price within the life of the put contract, the put will be exercised at the 33 price. The $550 received from the sale of the two options protects the writer against capital loss down to the level of $27\frac{1}{2}$ (33 minus $5\frac{1}{2}$). If the stock continues its rise through the expiration of the put, the call at 30 will be exercised, and the put will expire. The $550 collected from the two options protects the writer against capital loss to the price level of $35\frac{1}{2}$ (30 plus 3 plus $2\frac{1}{2}$).

Another possible defense for a naked call writer exists. If the stock rises by the amount of the original premium of $300 (or to any predetermined level), a naked straddle option can be sold at the higher level, thereby providing another, and larger, premium. The writer still has no stock position. If the stock subsequently declines to a lower price from the level at which the straddle was sold, the put will be exercised. The writer will then have 100 shares to deliver if called on the first call he wrote. Should the stock rise in price after issuing the straddle, the writer runs the risk of being called on 200 shares of stock—one call from the straddle issued and one call originally issued naked. The writer's protection in this case is limited to the original call premium plus the premium received for the naked straddle.

There is a fourth defensive strategy used by some sophisticated naked OTC call-option writers. If a stock underlying a naked call rises by the amount of the premium (or any predetermined amount), the writer can buy 100 shares at the higher level, and, if still bearish, try to *sell two additional calls* at the now higher level. The writer's belief is that, at this higher level, his judgment may be right. The stock hopefully will decline, and the calls issued at the higher level will expire. Should this happy sequence occur, the naked call writer can still be called at a lower level on the first call he wrote, but he will own 100 shares of stock and can deliver. The writer will have benefited in this situation from the three call premiums he received. With this strategy, however, the naked call writer still *bears the risk* that the stock may continue its rise even after his purchase of 100 shares and the issuance of two new calls.

There are still other ingenious methods of defending a naked OTC call option writer's position, such as buying offsetting calls. All these defenses require additional capital, and most of them involve additional liability. The naked OTC call-option writer must be aware that the defenses discussed herein *neither guarantee nor offer elimination of risk!*

Naked OTC call writing, of course, entails a high degree of risk for a potentially high return on capital. Naked OTC call writing requires frequent judgments and decisions. The practice definitely is *not suited for every option writer.* These techniques should be known and the strategies understood by any registered representative who wants to help prospects and clients attempt to earn a return from option-writing activities.

Bearish option writers sometimes write puts, even though the bulk of their option-writing is naked calls. If a bearish option writer does write a put, he *invariably sells stock short* at the time he writes the put. His hope and belief is that the stock will decline in price. Should that event occur, the put is then exercised. Stock bought through the forced purchase is then used to close out the short position. In this situation, the bearish writer nets the part of the put premium that remains after commission expenses for buying and shorting the stock.

The bearish writer who grants straddles believes that the stock underlying the straddle will go down in price. The premium being offered by the straddle buyer may appear enticing. In order to seek a premium profit in accordance with his negative view, he collateralizes the straddle by executing a short sale in the stock. If his judgment is correct and the stock declines, the put most certainly will be exercised. At the end of the time period, the put stock is used to close out the existing short position in the stock. This sequence allows the correct bearish straddle writer to earn that part of the straddle premium remaining after the commission expenses for shorting and buying the stock have been paid.

The bearish straddle and put writer is usually prepared to employ strategies available to him should his initial judgment prove wrong. The diligent registered representative must try to learn and master as many of these strategies and techniques as possible. The more knowledge he has, the more service he can provide to his clients.

14 OTC Option Hedge Writing

Ever since the concept of investing originated, investors have sought ways to put money to work that would incur *little risk* yet still offer a gain potential. As investing grew, the recognition also grew *that greater investment return is generally achieved only through greater investment risk.* Nonetheless, the search continues for investments that can offer a great potential return at low risk.

Some of those who issue option contracts for a living have tried to refine their option writing methods to eliminate as much risk as possible. One of these is the *hedge method.* This heretofore unnamed technique will be referred to as the "position one, sell two" method. This OTC option writing concept seems to present a lot of merit, and registered representatives should learn it to make available to well-capitalized option writing prospects and clients. This hedge method appears to enhance the gain potential of most option writers.

Of course, the intelligent investor and registered representative should realize that *there is no perfect investment.* No one investment or money management technique is better than all others at all times.

The "position one, sell two" method works thus. Assume that an OTC option writer is contacted and asked to supply call options on ZYX at 40, the current market price. The desired time frame is six months and ten days, and the premium being offered is $500. The stock is of medium volatility, and the premium is fairly typical for the time period.

The OTC hedge option writer would normally *buy 100 shares at 40 and issue two six-month, ten-day calls.* (A larger writer might buy 200 shares of stock and sell four calls, or buy five and sell ten, or whatever would be a normal transaction for the amount of his capital commitment to option writing.) The option writer in this example collects $1,000 in premiums from the sale of the two calls. He owns 100 shares of ZYX, which is readily available to deliver to the holder of one of the calls in case the stock rises above 40 and is called.

If the stock remains below the level of 40, neither call will be exercised at the end of the time period. The writer owns only

100 shares of stock. His stock position in ZYX at 40 is protected by the $1,000 premium he received from the sale of the two calls. Even if ZYX declines to the level of 30, *his own capital* is still intact. His risk in owning ZYX is in a decline below 30.

If the price of ZYX shares rises within the time period, the calls, in all probability, will be exercised. The writer has 100 shares originally bought at 40 and must make available another 100 shares to the holder of the second call.

How does the "position one, sell two" option writer limit risk in the event of a price increase of ZYX shares? He places an open order with the broker (for the time period involved), instructing the broker to *buy a second 100 shares* of ZYX if it rises to 50. The limit at 50 is derived by adding the premiums received from the sale of the two calls to the striking price (40 + 10). This buy-stop order will not be executed unless the stock makes this substantial move within the time period. If a price move of this magnitude does take place, the buy-stop is triggered, and the writer is forced to buy the second 100 shares of stock. At that point, the option writer has 200 shares available to deliver against the calls written at 40.

The "position one, sell two" option writer's viewpoint is that buying 100 shares of stock and selling two call options allows him to *achieve both up-side and down-side protection.* If ZYX stays between 30 and 50 during the time period, the writer will generally make money.

Of the major stock exchanges, only the New York Stock Exchange accepts buy-stop orders. If the hedge method is used on stocks other than New York Stock Exchange stocks, close watch must be maintained on the position in conjunction with a mental stop.

In the opinion of the "position one, sell two" option writer, most NYSE stocks generally do not swing out of the ranges described in six months and ten days' time. In our example, the writer has constructed a capital risk protection zone—a zone that extends 25 percent up and 25 percent down from the striking price. The *closer to the striking price the stock remains, the greater the profit to the option writer.*

The hedge option writer will usually try to select stocks that, in his opinion, will stay within the parameters of his protection limits and, hopefully, close to the striking price.

This hedge option writing strategy can only be used by a well-funded option writer, since it employs the concept of selling one call option covered and one call option naked. By issuing a naked call, the writer must meet the equity and naked option margin requirements of the New York Stock Exchange firm with which he is doing business.

The strategy of positioning one and selling two is most generally employed in the selling of OTC call options. However, it can easily be used for issuing partially covered OTC put options. The option writer, in the latter case, might sell 100 shares of stock short at 40 and issue two six-month, ten-day put options at $500 each (using the same striking price and premium as in our earlier hedge call writing example). The premiums he receives total $1,000. Should the stock go down, the writer will be put with 200 shares of stock. One hundred can be used to close out his short position. After being put and closing his short position, the writer is long 100 shares of ZYX at 40. This position is protected by the $1,000 he received from the two put premiums, giving the writer insurance down to the price level of 30 on ZYX.

After granting the two puts and selling 100 ZYX short at 40, what if there is a price rise that endures to the expiration of the puts? If this scenario occurs, the put options will expire unexercised. The writer will be at risk on only 100 shares of stock sold short. The short-sale risk carries the protection of the put premium receipt of $1,000.

The sophisticated hedge writer of puts protects himself against the theoretically unlimited risk of a short sale by placing a buy-stop order at 50. This serves to limit his possible short-sale loss.

These strategies are, as yet, little known in the investment industry. They have mainly been the province of knowledgeable option writers and a select few registered representatives. Such strategies can immensely enhance the profit search by investors and assist well-trained brokers to earn above-average income under almost any market conditions.

15 Common OTC Option Writing Problems and Possible Defenses

Registered representatives who handle option-writing accounts are sometimes going to be asked for their recommendations for defending a certain position or solving a particular problem that has arisen in an option writing portfolio. The situation might involve a problem facing a bullish option writer who has issued an OTC call option on a stock that is declining, or a bearish writer who has issued an OTC call on a rising stock. *Expect* these problems to arise. Learn the possible strategies to pursue in limiting loss.

Knowledge of this nature can make a registered representative an invaluable assistant to the investor. Through his option knowhow, the stockbroker can gain the respect of wealthy investors. His knowledge will serve to increase the number of referral prospects from satisfied clients. In the typical investor's eyes, the broker who knows the option business stands head and shoulders above his competitors.

Let's examine a typical problem for a bearish call writer and a strategy that might alleviate the problem. The bearish writer, as you will remember, generally issues calls and does not buy or own stock to collateralize the calls. He hopes the stock will not rise and remain above the strike within the life of his contracts. The bearish call writer also expects to avoid all commission expenses from every right judgment. If the OTC calls he issues are not exercised, he has no stock to buy or sell and, of course, no commissions to pay.

Sometimes, a bearish OTC option writer finds himself in a bind. The stock on which he has sold a naked call rises in price. Assume the following facts. An option writer with a negative opinion about ZYX sold a naked 95-day call on ZYX at 30 for $300. ZYX, despite his original negative viewpoint, promptly rises to 33, and the writer begins to fear that this rise may continue. What avenues are available to defend the position?

One possible defense entails the bearish writer's entering a buy-stop order at 33 (the strike plus premium is a general rule of thumb used by some sophisticated negative writers) to prevent an unlimited and unknown loss. If the buy-stop order is executed, the position is no longer naked. The drawback, of course, to this defense is that if the stock touches 33, triggering the buy order, it may later decline substantially. If that happens—the buy order is triggered and the stock then declines substantially—a second call can be issued *at the expiration of the first call.* This action serves to further reduce the option writer's risk in owning the stock.

A second potential defense is to simply remain naked on the call issued at 30 and *purchase an offsetting call* for the remaining period of time. This action limits any loss to the amount of the premium the writer pays for the offsetting call, plus commission expenses. Please note that present New York Stock Exchange rules will not allow the long call to margin the short call. The dollar risk would be checked, but margin is still required for the naked call position.

A third recourse for the naked OTC call writer who is faced with a rising stock is to enter a buy-stop order at 33, as in our first mentioned defense. If this buy-stop is executed and the writer's opinion is still bearish, he can attempt to sell a second, 95-day call for approximately $325 at the new, higher level (if a call bid can be found). If the stock declines from the higher level, the writer will have received *two premiums,* totaling $625, and he'll *own only 100* shares of stock. If the first call, written at 30, is exercised and the second is not, he will have 100 shares of stock to deliver and will wind up the transactions with a profit.

The possibility also exists that after the buy-stop order is triggered at the 33 price and the second call is issued, the stock may later decline to below 30 without either call being exercised. In that scenario, the writer's capital is then at risk only if the stock declines below 26¾ (assuming that the second call premium was sold for $325 at the 33 level).

Still another defense for the naked OTC call writer is to sell a put option at 33 (if a bid is available) for 95 days. A normal premium in this case is approximately $275. If the stock declines from the 33 level, the put will be exercised. The writer will own 100 shares of stock at the 33 price and *will have received two premiums, totaling $575.* Upon exercise of the put, the writer's new long position is protected by the premiums to a level of 27¼. If the writer is *put at 33* and *then later called,* on the call issued at 30, he will have made a profit. If, after selling the put at 33, the stock continues to rise, the writer has *increased his protection against loss* to the level of 35¾. The premiums used in this example are normal for medium-volatility stocks in the OTC option market at the current time.

16 Defending a Bullish OTC Call Option Writer's Position

Bullish OTC call writers are often faced with the problem of stock price declines in their long positions. Defending their positions becomes of major importance and is not easily accomplished. Let's assume the following facts. A bullish OTC call writer bought 100 shares of ZYX at 40. The shares were used to back a call option issued for six months and ten days for a premium of $500. ZYX declines in price to 35, and at that level the writer is no longer bullish, but he fears that the decline may continue and the call expire unexercised.

One defense available to the writer in this situation is to sell the 100 shares of ZYX at the 35 level and *remain naked*. If this is done, prudence should dictate the placing of a *buy-stop order at the strike price* so that the stock position will be reinstated if his judgment in going naked proves wrong and a turnaround develops. This strategy works very well in a declining market and serves to prevent large losses that might occur if a position is simply held continuously. The drawback is, of course, the whipsaw. Bullish OTC call writers who practice this system, however, believe the *risk in the whipsaw is much less dangerous* and *less frequent* than that of a substantial stock price decline. Of course, the writer must be capitalized sufficiently to meet whatever house requirements are necessary to go naked.

A second defense possibility for the bullish OTC call writer faced with a declining stock is to *sell 100 ZYX* and *buy a call* on 100 ZYX to cover the remaining time of exposure. In this case, the writer should try to *buy a call near the striking price* and above the current market *due to the lower cost of such an option*. His loss will be limited to the amount paid for the above-the-market call. If this out-of-the-money call cannot be purchased, he should buy a call at the market price.

A third defense posture is to issue a *second call option* on ZYX at the *35 level* for a premium of approximately $425 (if a bid is available). If the second call can be successfully consummated, the writer has to make a judgment about the risk for the remaining time in granting two call options secured by only 100 shares of stock.

Writers who choose to defend themselves by issuing a second call believe that the second premium received against the 100-share position might make the entire transaction profitable. As a further protection, they will usually *try to limit the risk* they would incur with a sharp price recovery by entering a buy-stop order with their broker to purchase a second 100 shares of ZYX at the original strike price, which, in our example, was 40. Please note that *if neither call is exercised,* the *writer is protected* to a level of 30¾. At the expiration of both calls, he might sell still a third call option, thereby taking in another premium. Should the second call option issued at 35 be exercised and the first call expire, the transactions produce a profit. The possibility also exists that if the buy stop order at 40 is executed, both calls might be exercised. Even if this occurs, the writer still earns a profit on the combined results of the transactions.

17 Defending the Bullish OTC Put Writer's Position

Bullish put writing involves issuing put contracts with cash reserved to pay for the stock if it declines and the put contract is exercised. One incentive for bullish put writers whose judgments prove correct is that they *entirely avoid the commission expenses* involved in buying and selling stock.

The problem they encounter most often is that of a price decline in a stock upon which they have issued a put. Assume the following facts. A bullish OTC put writer grants a 95-day put contract on ZYX at 50, for a $500 premium. Early in the contract life, ZYX declines to 45, and the writer's opinion changes from bullish to bearish. He now fears a further price drop. What defenses can he use in this, or similar, situations?

One defense is to sell 100 shares of ZYX short at 45. If the short sale can be arranged and executed, the writer can also place a buy-stop order to purchase 100 shares to cover the short sale at 45 (50 was the original strike). If the writer's bearish suspicions turn out to be correct, the put will be exercised and the stock bought through the put can then be used to close out the short sale. On a wrong initial judgment, the writer's loss can be held down to approximate the commission expense.

If the writer still feels reasonably bullish about the stock despite the price drop, he can take another line of defense. He can issue a naked, 95-day call option at the 45 strike for a premium of approximately $400 (if a bid is available). If the put at 50 is exercised, the writer will own 100 shares of stock that will fully back the call issued at 45. Should the call at 45 also be exercised, the writer would obtain a profit in a situation where his original judgment was wrong.

A third defense posture is to *sell 100 shares of ZYX short at 45* and *buy* an above-the-market *call* at the strike price of 50 for the remaining time of the put. This defense *limits the loss* to the amount paid for the above-the-market call and also *prevents any possible whipsaw* from creating a substantial loss. Above-the-market call options are generally available at *much lower prices* than market options. If an above-the-market call cannot readily be obtained, the writer can purchase a call at the market price of the stock.

18 Defending the Bearish OTC Put Writer's Position

Occasionally, a registered representative will come in contact with a bearish OTC put writer. Bearish OTC put writing is uncommon because the commission expenses involved, along with the generally lower premiums for OTC puts, make the strategy economically unrewarding. There are market periods, however, when put premiums become equal to, or greater than, call premiums. When such conditions occur, bearish OTC put writing may become attractive.

Assume the following facts. A bearish OTC put writer sells 100 ZYX short at 40. The time period is six months and ten days. The premium collected by the writer is $500. In this situation, the writer's hope and belief is that the stock will decline and the put be exercised. If that sequence occurs, the put stock will be used to close the short position. The writer will have earned the portion of the premium remaining after commission expenses.

Shortly after issuing the put and shorting the stock, however, ZYX rises to 45 and the writer begins to fear that the upward movement may continue and the put will expire unexercised, leaving him with his existing short position. What possible defenses are available to the writer in this situation?

Acting upon his reassessment, the writer can try to protect himself by buying 100 ZYX at 45 to cover the short position. This leaves him with a naked put outstanding at 40. If the stock remains at 40 or above, the only loss on the initial wrong judgment is the commission expenses incurred in shorting and covering.

If, after buying ZYX at 45 to cover the short stock position, ZYX falls to the 40 range, the writer (if bearish again) can enter a new short-sale order near the 40 level to take care of the potential put liability. The whipsaw is believed by many bearish OTC put writers to be *less dangerous* and *less frequent* than the risk of a substantial price rise.

A second line of defense available to the bearish OTC put writer is to buy 100 ZYX at 45 to cover the short position. Simultaneous with covering the short, the writer can buy a below-the-market put on ZYX at 40 for the remaining time period. After taking these two steps, the writer cannot lose more than the amount paid for the below-the-market put and the cost of commissions in shorting and covering.

A third possibility for our bearish OTC put writer who changes his opinion on the outlook for ZYX is to *sell a second six-month, ten-day put* on ZYX at 45 for approximately $550. The writer, in this case, is making a risk judgment for the remaining time in having issued two put options against a short position of only 100 shares of stock. The writer who subscribes to this defense believes that by accepting the second premium, the entire transaction might work out profitably. Should neither put be exercised, the writer will be protected on his short sale at 40 (by the two put premiums he received, totaling $1,050) to a level of 50½. At the expiration of the first put, he might be able to *sell a third put option,* further extending the up-side protection for his short position. If the second put is exercised and the first put option expires, the transaction will be profitable because the short position can be closed out by delivering the put stock.

A writer would normally attempt to limit the risk of a stock price decline in this situation by placing another short-sale order at the 40 level after the second put option is issued.

19 New York Stock Exchange Rules and Regulations Governing Option Transactions

The New York Stock Exchange has formulated several rules regarding options. This chapter discusses the most important of them. Every registered representative who handles option-trading accounts must become thoroughly familiar with these rules.

Rule 431(d)(2): Puts, Calls, and Other Options

No put or call carried for a customer shall be considered of any value for the purpose of computing the margin required in the account of such customer.

This simply means that an option owned by a client *has no loan value,* even if, through sale, or exercise and liquidation, a value were to be obtained.

The issuance or guarantee for a customer of a put or a call shall be considered as a security transaction subject to paragraph (a)[1] of this Rule.

---

[1] *Rule 431(a): Initial Margin Rule.* For the purpose of effecting new securities transactions and commitments, the margin required shall be an amount equivalent to the requirements of paragraph (b) of this Rule, or such greater amount as the Exchange may from time to time require for specific securities, with a minimum equity in the account of at least $2,000, except that cash need not be deposited in excess of the cost of any security purchased. The foregoing minimum equity and cost of purchase provisions shall not apply to "when distributed" securities in cash accounts and the exercise of rights to subscribe.

For the purpose of this Rule, the term *customer* shall include any person or entity for whom securities are purchased or sold or to whom securities are sold or from whom securities are purchased whether on a regular way, when-issued, delayed or future delivery basis. It will also include any person or entity for whom securities

For the purpose of paragraph (b)[2] of this Rule such puts and calls shall be considered as if they were exercised.

Each such put or call shall be margined separately and any difference between the market price and the price of a put or call shall be considered to be of value only in providing the amount of margin required on that particular put or call.

If both a put and a call for the same number of shares of the same security are issued or guaranteed for a customer, the amount of margin required shall be the margin on the put or call, whichever is greater.

Where a call is issued or guaranteed against an existing "long" position or a put is issued or guaranteed against an existing "short" position, no margin need be required on the call or put, provided such "long" or "short" position is adequately margined in accordance with this Rule. In computing margin on such existing stock position carried against a put or call, the current market price to be used shall not be greater than the call price in the case of a call or less than the put price in the case of a put.

When a member, or member organization issues or guarantees

---

are held or carried. The term will not include a broker or dealer from whom a security has been purchased or to whom a security has been sold for the account of the member organization or its customers.

Withdrawals of cash or securities may be made from any account which has a debit balance, "short" position, or commitments, provided that after such withdrawal the equity in the account is at least the greater of $2,000 or the amount required by the maintenance requirement of this Rule.

[Author's note: An OTC option owned by a client may be withdrawn or delivered out of the account even if the account is restricted.]

[2] *Rule 431(b): Maintenance Margin Rule.* The margin which must be maintained in margin accounts of customers whether members, allied members, member organizations or non-members, shall be as follows:

(1) 25% of the market value of all securities "long" in the account;
[Author's note: Uncovered puts are treated as "long" positions; therefore, the minimum margin requirement for endorsing a put is 25% plus or minus the difference between market and strike.]
plus

(2) $2.50 per share or 100% of the market value, in cash, whichever amount is greater, of each stock "short" in the account selling at less than $5.00 per share; plus

(3) $5.00 per share or 30% of the market value, in cash, whichever amount is greater, of each stock "short" in the account selling at $5.00 per share or above;

[Author's note: Uncovered calls (naked calls) are treated as short positions; therefore, the minimum margin requirement for endorsing a naked call is 30% of the market plus or minus the difference between market and strike.]
plus

(4) 5% of the principal amount or 30% of the market value, in cash, whichever amount is greater, of each bond "short" in the account.

an option to receive or deliver securities for a customer, such option shall be margined as if it were a put or call.

Rule 367: Deliveries on Privileges.

When securities are received or delivered for an allied member or a non-member on a privilege, full non-member commissions shall be charged and collected.

This simply means that a commission on the underlying stock will be charged to a client upon exercise of an option.

Rule 381 (20): Sale of Profitable Options
Owned by Customers.

When a member organization sells for the account of a customer, or buys from such customer, a profitable option, the member organization shall charge such customer two commissions.

This rule was formulated prior to the existence of the CBOE. The *profitable options* referred to are OTC options.

Registered representatives who handle, or intend to handle, active option writing accounts should confer with their particular margin departments to gain a complete understanding of house option margin requirements.

II The CBOE Option Market

20 Introduction to the Chicago Board Options Exchange

April 26, 1973 was a day that may well go down in investors' diaries as the beginning of a new era for the securities industry. This day marked the opening of trading on the Chicago Board Options Exchange. This new exchange made call-option contracts available for the first time to the investing public in an auction market procedure. Price visibility as to the high, low, last, and volume of each contract traded became instantly available through desk-top terminals located in almost every brokerage office.

The Chicago Board Options Exchange was created through the efforts of the Chicago Board of Trade. It took almost five years and approximately $2.5 million in capital to realize this concept and get the new exchange on its feet, but now a new opportunity market for investors and registered representatives alike is available for participation.

Since the Chicago Board option differs greatly from the OTC option, it is important for interested registered representatives to learn all the facts and facets of this new and exciting investment medium. The strategies available to the buyers and writers of CBOE options are almost without limit. Some of these new strategies and possibilities will be discussed in the following chapters.

Before delving into the CBOE option trading techniques, however, one must familiarize himself with the language used in trading CBOE options. The process by which orders are executed in this market are *entirely different* from the OTC option market. That, too, must be learned, both by the registered representative and the investor.

The Chicago Board Options Exchange contract was the first option transaction ever to gain network radio and television coverage, and its contract was the first ever to be executed through an open, competitive bidding situation on a national securities exchange.

In order to popularize option trading, the Chicago Board Options Exchange had to cure some of the problems that exist in the over-the-counter option market. One such problem in the OTC option market is the multiplicity of expiration dates. OTC options can expire on any one of 250-odd business days of the year. CBOE option contracts can only expire on one of four business days. The CBOE decided to *standardize expiration dates* and reduce the number of possible expiration dates, thereby simplifying record keeping for the buyers, writers, brokers, and the exchange.

In an effort to keep the *elements of the contract simple*, the CBOE also instituted standardized striking prices (exercise prices) in its contracts as compared with the infinite variety of striking price possibilities that exist with over-the-counter option contracts.

To insure the performance of contracts, a clearing house was established to serve as writer to all buyers and buyer to all writers. This clearing house actually severed the relationship between the original buyer and writer of an option. The clearing house is funded by deposits of clearing members and collects margin deposits or security deposits from writing members. Clearing house settlements of money due or owed are made the next day.

These improvements simplified option trading and serve to reduce the variables in an option basically to one—the option price or premium. This premium is expected to vary up or down as the stock price moves up and down and as time dwindles from the option life.

One main objective of the CBOE is to provide a marketplace for trading option contracts that has continuity, that has liquidity. (In other words, it functions as a secondary system by which buyers or writers can dispose of their contracts or obligations much like the trading that goes on in any listed security today.) This *introduction of an organized secondary market for options* makes possible many different strategies and techniques. It is through this secondary market that writers or buyers can eliminate or liquidate their positions by making an offsetting transaction on the CBOE.

From the commodity market the CBOE borrowed the futures concept of delivery months. The acronym JAJO is easy for the registered representative to remember. It stands for the expiration dates of all CBOE contracts. The last business days of January, April, July, or October are the only expiration dates for which a CBOE contract can be written. Starting with the July 1974 contracts, the expiration of CBOE contracts will be at 10:30 a.m. on the last Monday of each expiration month. If Monday is a holiday, the expiration day will be the next business day after the last Monday.

The registered representative soliciting clients to participate in CBOE option trading must be aware that a prospectus must be delivered to each client who wants to buy or sell CBOE contracts. In addition, the customer must declare in writing that he *will not violate certain limits* in terms of contracts on the CBOE. A manual made available by the CBOE, entitled *Managing Customer Accounts on the Chicago Board Options Exchange,* contains information concerning the handling of clients' accounts on this exchange. Every registered representative who decides to enter into this business must thoroughly familiarize himself with this CBOE manual.

21 CBOE Call-Option Buying Strategy

The liquidity, or secondary market feature, of the CBOE call option is perhaps the *most significant difference* between that option and an OTC option. This unique advantage builds a very strong case for buying call options on the CBOE.

Assume that an investor is intrigued with the up-side possibilities in XYZ over the next six months. The current price of XYZ stock is 30, and call options are available in both the OTC option market and the CBOE for a premium cost of $400. The speculator purchases XYZ six-month calls in both the OTC and CBOE option markets. One month after purchase, XYZ rises in price to $33 per share. On the OTC call option, the investor is glad that the stock price is up, but he really *can't derive a profit benefit* from the price advance. If he were to exercise his call to buy at 30 and sold out in the open market at 33, he would regain $300, less commissions, from his premium risk of $400. That certainly would not be a very satisfactory result. His course, then, is either to hope for the stock to continue upward or to trade against the OTC call as outlined in the OTC call-buying chapter.

With the CBOE call option on the same stock, the investor can look forward to a quite different possibility upon a price increase of three points in XYZ one month after the purchase of his six-month call. He can *sell the call contract on the CBOE.* With the stock three points over the strike price and five months' life remaining, he should receive something greater than the difference between market price and strike price. This additional increment represents the *time value* remaining in the option. He can sell his option for perhaps $600 to $700, netting for himself a very handsome return on his risk capital after commission expenses. This liquidity feature is one that every registered representative should promote as one of the *most advantageous aspects* of trading options on the CBOE— a feature that can help clients in their two-fold goal of trying to limit risk and earn profits.

In the *OTC call-buying strategy* chapter, we pointed out that for an investor to have a reasonable chance for success in a call-buying program, he should envision a *price move* in the underlying stock of generally *three times the premium at risk.* This is a necessary precaution when trading in OTC call options from the buy side. On the CBOE, however, *small price moves in the underlying stock can generate very large percentage gains* for the call-option buyer. Many times, a price move of two or three points in the underlying stock can produce a 40 to 50 percent or more gain in the option, which can then be sold on the CBOE and the profit actually realized.

Because of the market-maker system on the CBOE, a continuous market for options is constantly available (although under certain conditions, option trading can be halted by the CBOE, just as halts occur in listed stock), and *options can be bought or sold even if no public buyer or seller is available.*

The ability to resell option contracts at any time on the CBOE serves to limit option losses as well as to make profits available with less stock price movement than in the OTC market. In our example, had the stock declined from 30 to 27, the CBOE call option holder could have still sold his option contract for a value on that exchange. He would have gotten less, certainly, than what he paid originally, but he would have been able to get out of his contract and retain some portion of his premium. The holder of an OTC option contract can rarely, if ever, obtain any reasonable value for the time remaining in his option contract. In the OTC option market, it is extremely difficult to sell a call option with the market price below the strike price.

The CBOE call option, like its brother, the OTC call option, can be traded against. Short sales can be made fully protected and insured by the CBOE call, just as outlined in Chapter 3. CBOE calls can also be used to protect an initial short position in the underlying stock.

An investor who believes a stock price decline is going to occur in a particular stock (yet wanting to insure himself against a wrong judgment), might well buy a CBOE call and simultaneously short the stock. Should the stock fall as much as he anticipates, he will earn a fine, short-term, capital gain, reduced by the expense of the CBOE call premium. If the short stock position were to go against him, his risk would be limited to his commission expense and the cost of the CBOE call.

This strategy, however, *is not ordinarily appealing to investors,* as it requires, in addition to the option premium, collateralization of the short sale and the expense of commissions on the underlying stock. Should the stock rise, any call gains would be offset by the short-sale loss. A more viable alternative for the negative investor is to purchase on OTC put option. Trading in CBOE put options is expected to begin sometime in 1974.

The CBOE call option's *biggest attraction for buyers* is the possibility of very large percentage gains on the premium risk within very short time periods. The CBOE is an exciting and much faster trading market than the OTC option market because of its liquidity feature.

CBOE options can be bought for time periods of over six months. The investor who buys and then sells a CBOE contract at a profit after holding it for over six months earns long-term capital gains, just as with an OTC call option.

Registered representatives, of course, must always keep in mind that *suitability for the client is of primary importance*. No client should be encouraged to commit more than a small percentage of his assets to buying options because he runs the *risk of losing 100 percent of his investment* if his judgment is wrong. Therefore, any investor should buy only in the amount he can really afford to risk.

22 Chicago Board Options Exchange Listing Requirements and Terms

In April 1973, the new Chicago Board Options Exchange began trading in call options on sixteen stocks. Because the advent of this new exchange may quite conceivably change trading patterns in the securities industry, it is important for registered representatives and investors alike to learn the essential details about the CBOE. This knowledge must include the risk possibilities as well as the reward potential.

The volume on the CBOE has been in excess of the expectations of its founders. "Bulls" on the future of this exchange believe that sometime in the not too distant future, trading, as measured in terms of underlying shares, on the exchange might possibly rival that of the New York Stock Exchange.

Before option trading can begin on the CBOE, the stock underlying the option must meet certain eligibility requirements for listing. The principal listing guidelines are as follows.

1. There must be a *minimum of 10 million registered, outstanding shares.* Eighty percent of these outstanding shares have to be held by the general public, that is, by those individuals or corporations who *do not* have to file their holdings with the Securities and Exchange Commission.

2. There must be a *minimum of 10,000 shareholders of record.*

3. *Minimum trading volume must be at least 1 million* shares for *each* of the two previous years on the principal exchange where the stock is listed.

4. *Minimum price is $10 per share* at the time the stock is approved for option trading on the CBOE.

In addition to these criteria for the stock itself, the corporation that issues the stock must meet certain requirements.

1. *A majority of the board of directors* of the company being admitted to option trading on the CBOE must have been directors

of the company (or its predecessor) for the three previous fiscal years.

2. During the past ten years, the company *must not have been in default* on long-lease rental payments, sinking fund installments, preferred stock dividends, or bond or debenture interest.

3. *The company must have earned,* after taxes, at least $500,000 a year for the five years prior to listing (before extraordinary gains or losses).

4. *The company must have earned* all dividends paid on all classes of securities for the five fiscal years prior to listing (including fair market value of any stock dividend).

The Chicago Board Options Exchange originally intended to have option trading in 100 stocks or more by the end of 1973. However, certain problems in the initial months caused this goal to be reduced to approximately 60. One problem area was the *general under-capitalization and lack of experience* of many of the market-makers. Another problem was associated with the relative *slowness of the price reporting* and *price dissemination procedures.* Still another problem was the relatively cramped floor facility, combined with *more than expected volume.* Exchange officials recognize these problems and are undertaking *corrective steps to solve them* and thereby pave the way for even greater trading volume. In good time, after the Chicago Board Options Exchange has gained experience and its market-makers are strengthened, it plans to begin trading in put contracts too.

The CBOE call option is really a new type of security with exclusive characteristics and features. It is the result of a combination of the *best features of a commodity futures contract* with the *best features of an option contract.* Eliminated to the greatest extent were the *worst features of both.* This modern security vehicle should provide a very unique instrument to seek profits while holding risk in check.

Registered representatives who hope to increase their business through the possibilities that exist in this new market must learn the terms that are used in connection with Chicago Board Options Exchange contracts. The following list includes the most frequently used terms and their definitions.

TYPE OF OPTION: A put contract or a call contract.

CLASS OF OPTIONS: All option contracts of the same *type* covering the same underlying security.

SERIES OF OPTIONS: All option contracts of the same class having the same exercise price and the same expiration date.

EXERCISE PRICE: The specified price at which the underlying security may be bought or sold upon the exercise of an option contract (subject to certain adjustments as per the terms of the contract).

AGGREGATE EXERCISE PRICE: The exercise price of an option contract multiplied by the number of units of the underlying security covered by the option contract.

UNDERLYING SECURITY: The security that the Clearing Corporation of the Chicago Board Options Exchange is obligated to sell (in the case of a call option) or buy (in the case of a put option) upon the valid exercise of an option contract.

PRIMARY MARKET: The principal market in which the underlying security of an option contract is traded.

LONG POSITION: An investor's interest as a *holder* of units of trading of a given option contract.

SHORT POSITION: An investor's interest as a writer of one or more units of trading of a given option contract.

COVERED: A short position in an option contract where the writer's obligation is *secured* by a specific deposit or an escrow deposit; or the writer holds a long position in the underlying security or securities convertible into the underlying security.

UNCOVERED: A short position in an option contract that is not covered by a position in the underlying security or its equivalent.

OPENING PURCHASE TRANSACTION: A CBOE transaction that will create or increase *a long position* in an option contract.

OPENING WRITING TRANSACTION: A CBOE transaction that will create or increase *a short position* in an option contract.

CLOSING PURCHASE TRANSACTION: A CBOE transaction that will reduce or eliminate a short position in an option contract.

CLOSING WRITING TRANSACTION: A CBOE transaction that will reduce or eliminate a long position on an option contract.

OUTSTANDING: An option contract that was issued by the Clearing Corporation of the CBOE and has neither been the subject of a closing writing transaction nor has reached its expiration date.

23 Orders, Commissions, and Price Information on the CBOE

Interest in the CBOE is building throughout the investment community, interest that is being stimulated by ads and member-firm educational seminars run by this new exchange. Public investor interest, in turn, is being created through planned promotions by various member firms. Their promotional efforts run the gamut from newspaper ads, radio and TV commercials, to public seminars and heavy direct-mail campaigns. This impetus and exposure added to a proven viability of the product *may very well lead to a giant trading market*.

Registered representatives should acquaint themselves with the kinds of orders that are permitted, the commission costs that are involved, and how price information is disseminated. Familiarity with these aspects of CBOE option trading may well enable a perceptive broker and investor to take advantage of price disparities and opportunities that may be available in this new securities market.

Orders

MARKET ORDER. This order is accepted by all firms participating in the Chicago Board Options Exchange. It's simply an order to buy or sell a stated number of contracts at the best possible price whenever the order reaches the post. *Caution:* The option market is much "thinner" than the stock market, so great care should be taken if entering market orders. If it is a large, multiple-lot order, a limit order, described next, is probably most prudent.

LIMIT ORDER. This order also should be accepted by all participating members of the CBOE and is simply an order to buy or sell a stated number of option contracts at a specified price *or better*.

CONTINGENCY ORDER. A contingency order is a limit or market order to buy or sell that is contingent upon satisfaction of a specified condition while the order is at the post. *Please note that some members of the Chicago Board Options Exchange will not accept certain contingency orders.*

Market-if-Touched Order. The market-if-touched (MIT) order is a contingency order to buy or sell when the market for a particular option contract reaches a specified price.

Stop Order. This order is often referred to as a stop-loss order; it is a contingency order to buy or sell at the market when the market for a particular option reaches a specified price. *Use with care.*

Stop-Limit Order. Stop-limit order is a contingency order to buy or sell at a *limited price* when the market for a particular option contract reaches a specified price. Most members of the Chicago Board Options Exchange will accept these orders. *Caution*: This order does not guarantee an execution, as the price limit may prove restrictive.

Spread Order. A spread order is an order to buy a particular option contract and to sell another option contract at some specified differential between the two. *Caution:* Before entering this order, *check carefully your CBOE member firm's margin requirements* on this transaction.

Not-Held Order. A not-held order is a market order that gives the broker on the floor of the CBOE *discretion as to the price or time* at which the order is to be executed.

One-Cancels-the-Other Order. This order, often referred to as an OCO order, consists of two or more orders treated as a unit. The execution of any one of the orders causes the others to be cancelled. Some member firms of the Chicago Board Options Exchange will not accept orders of this type.

The registered representative must be familiar with his firm's order policy. Most firms will take orders good through various time periods, orders such as good for the week, good for the month, good through a specific date. These orders are known as open orders. The bulk of the orders entered on the Chicago Board Options Exchange are market, limit, and spread orders.

One of the prime advantages to investors trading on the CBOE is that the commission charge *is lower* than that associated with the equivalent amount of the underlying stock. The CBOE's commission structure provides for a *minimum commission* on every option order executed on the exchange for non-members. If the money involved in the order is over $100, the minimum commission is $25 or the applicable commission schedule of the principal stock exchanges, *whichever is higher*. The CBOE commission is based upon three factors: (1) The *price of the option* rather than the price of the underlying stock; (2) the *total premium dollar amount* involved in the trade; and (3) the *number of contract units* involved in the trade.

Computations as to commission costs for a particular trade can be made by using the following information from the CBOE Commission Schedule.

SINGLE TRADING UNIT ORDERS

Money Involved in the Order [a]	Minimum Commission [b]
$ 100 – 2,499	1.3% + $12.00
$2,500 and above	0.9% + $22.00

[a] When the amount involved in an order is less than $100, the minimum commission is mutually agreed upon.

[b] The minimum commission on a single trading unit order may not be less than $25 nor more than $65.

MULTIPLE TRADING UNIT ORDERS

Money Involved in the Order [a]	Minimum Commissions [b]
$ 100 – 2,499	1.3% + $12.00
$ 2,500 – 19,999	0.9% + $22.00
$20,000 – 29,999	0.6% + $82.00
plus:	
First to tenth trading unit	$6.00 per trading unit
Eleventh trading unit and over	$4.00 per trading unit

[a] When the amount involved in an order is less than $100, the minimum commission is mutually agreed upon.

[b] The minimum commission per trading unit on multiple trading unit orders may not be more than the commission applicable to that unit if it were a single trading unit.

A commission increase of 10% for orders under $5,000 and 15% for those over $5,000 was permitted in late 1973.

CBOE rules also permit negotiation of commissions if the dollar amount of the order is in excess of $30,000. This compares with a $300,000 threshold for negotiation on stock transactions on the principal stock exchanges. The initial prospectus pointed out that for order amounts under $100, commissions would be as "mutually agreed." Most firms charge a minimum of $12.50 per order on these very small dollar amounts. Varied commission schedules prevail when options are traded for less than $100 each.

Registered representatives should note that, unlike commodity option commissions, CBOE contracts call for the commission to be charged upon the *opening of the position* and upon the *closing of the position.*

A great benefit and advantage over the OTC option market is the price dissemination arranged for by the Chicago Board Options Exchange. Price information on options traded on the CBOE is carried over Bunker-Ramo, Scantlin, and Ultronic terminals, usually available in brokerage offices. These desk-top units can be interrogated to retrieve the open, high, low, last, and previous close prices; volume; and elapsed time since the last trade. This information greatly aids the investor in decision making and serves to speed up executions and increase market depth. Daily and weekly newspapers carry reports of the CBOE trades so that "comparison shopping" is available to the investor.

All kinds of statistics on CBOE options and the underlying stocks are furnished to member firms by the CBOE. The interested registered representative can easily gain access to this information and make it available to his *clients* and *prospects.* The additional service can be a helpful stimulant to business.

24 Floor Brokers, Board Brokers, and Market-Makers: Order Executors on the CBOE

The eyes of the investment world continue to focus on the CBOE. The volume generated during its initial life confounded and amazed its detractors. What started off as a pilot operation appears ready to blossom into a much enlarged securities market if all goes according to the founders. One factor aiding in the growth of this exchange is the division of specialist duties in executing orders on the floor of the CBOE. The registered representative should have a clear understanding of how orders get executed and who handles them.

The *floor broker* is a registered member of the CBOE whose duty is to accept and execute orders received from members of the CBOE. A floor broker *cannot accept an order from any other source* (except under a very special circumstance). The floor broker has to pass a special examination and is charged with the responsibility of handling an order—execution at the best price available to him. He may handle orders such as contingency orders, limit orders, and market orders. *A floor broker is never permitted to execute discretionary orders*. (Such orders leave "to the discretion" of a broker factors such as the choice of the class of option to be bought or sold or the number of option contracts to be bought or sold.)

The *board broker* is an individual member or a nominee of a member who is registered with the CBOE for the purpose of acting as a "broker's broker" for specific classes of options. He accepts and attempts to execute orders placed with him by other members. He also is charged with the duty of monitoring the market for such classes of options at the post. Like the floor broker, the board broker must subscribe to the rules of the exchange, pass a written examination, and have a record of high standards of business conduct.

As part of his duties, the board broker must, for all option contracts of the class or classes to which his appointment extends, *accept* and *maintain* a *written record* of orders that are placed with him. Such orders can include market orders, limit orders, and any other orders that may be designated by the floor procedure committee of the CBOE.

The board broker *cannot under any circumstances accept orders of any other type or from any other source than a member.* A board broker or a temporary board broker, designated in accordance with a CBOE rule, must be at the post *not later than one-half hour before the opening* of the market each business day, and he must remain on the floor throughout the business day and for *at least fifteen minutes following the close* of the market (unless some unusual circumstance causes the floor procedure committee to require his presence for longer periods before the opening and after the close).

The board broker must make his best effort to execute the orders placed with him at the best price available to him under the rules of the exchange. The board broker is empowered to call upon market-makers who are appointed to act as specialists in a particular class of option contracts. These specialists must make bids and/or offers to standards set forth by the CBOE; this is an effort to maintain an ongoing, fluid, option market at *prices that narrow the gap between bids and offers.* A board broker also must, as part of his duties, report any unusual activity, or transaction, or price changes, to a floor official. He must also continuously display the *highest bid* and the *lowest offer,* along with the *number of option contracts bid for* at the highest bid and *offered* at the lowest offer in his book, in each option contract for which he is acting as board broker.

Market-makers are risk-taking individuals who are registered with the CBOE for the purpose of making transactions as dealer specialists on the floor of the CBOE. As with the other brokers on the floor, the market-maker must pass an examination and have a business history acceptable to the CBOE prior to being appointed market-maker. Additionally, he must have the financial resources to make the market in his class of options.

For some stock options there may be a team of market-makers working as a market-making unit. For the purposes of CBOE rules and procedures, a market-maker unit is treated as a single market-maker. The function of a market-maker is to make dealings that are calculated to contribute to the *making of a fair and orderly market.*

No market-maker should enter into any transaction or make bids or offers that are inconsistent with such a course of dealings.

The market-maker is expected to trade for his own account whenever a lack of price continuity exists, or when there is a temporary disparity between the supply and demand for a particular option contract, or when a distortion between the price relationships between option contracts of the same class occurs.

If called upon by a board broker to improve the market or make a bid or offer, or both, *he must do so* in accordance with the CBOE rules for providing a fair and orderly market. Generally, the market-maker may make a bid or offer to create a difference of *no more than one half of one dollar* between the bid and offer for each option contract for which the last transaction price was less than $20. He must make a bid or offer where there's *no more than a $1* spread between the bid and offer when the last preceding transaction price was over $20.

Market-makers *should not dominate the market* in option contracts of a particular class, either individually or as a group, whether intentionally or unintentionally. The market-maker *cannot act as a floor broker* on the *same business day* and in the *same class* of option contracts if he *also acts as a market-maker that day.* The only exception is if he is called upon by the board broker to improve a market situation.

No market-maker can hold an interest, or participate, in any joint account for the purpose of buying or selling any option contract unless that joint account is a *member* or member organization of the CBOE. Such an account must also be reported to, and not disapproved by, the CBOE. All these rules are, of course, established to implement a *viable, fast-moving option market* and to eliminate abuses and excesses that might otherwise occur.

One problem that faced the CBOE in its early months was the *lack of effectiveness of many of its market-makers.* Some appointed market-makers lacked experience and became so timid through early losses that they became reluctant to bid for, or offer, more than one contract unit. This, of course, made for a thin market, a market punctuated by relatively wide price gaps. CBOE officials have redoubled their efforts to obtain strongly capitalized, more experienced market-makers. This need has to be filled if the CBOE stock option list is to grow and its business expand.

25 CBOE Day Trading

OTC put and call dealers were virtually all astounded by the volume of option contracts traded on the new CBOE—a volume of trading that was accomplished in a stock market atmosphere marked by declining prices and lackluster volume. If volume follows the expansion of listing, then new, high levels of activity will be seen. Investors, speculators, and brokerage firms have taken to this new trading vehicle like a duck to water. Each new CBOE prospectus will probably provide new names of companies that may qualify for stock option trading on the CBOE.

The boy scout motto, *Be prepared*, should be foremost in the registered representative's mind when he explains the risks and rewards of CBOE trading to potential users. A problem area that should be clearly explained is one that relates to market orders. On the CBOE, market orders are often entered, and *executions obtained, at prices substantially away from previous sales*. This can happen if the underlying stock has made a substantial move and the option does not trade during the time period of the stock's move. Investors must be made fully aware that this can, and does, happen.

Financial Weekly and *Barron's* recap option-trading activity on the new Chicago Board Options Exchange. This recap can help the stockbroker and his clients to spotlight past moves and compare relative values.

This new exchange offers risk-oriented, aggressive speculators the opportunity to day trade options. Many CBOE options have experienced as much as *50 percent or greater upward price moves in a single day*. A significant number of options have *doubled or more in one day*. Also, a large number of options have *declined more than 50% in one trading session*. Option trading, like all security trading, is a two-way street!

A day trader at most member firms will find it necessary to have the *full price* of the option contract paid, *including commission cost*, in order to be able to liquidate a position the same day. Some member firms of the New York Stock Exchange permit CBOE day trades whereby a client can *sell* the option, perhaps early in the day, and buy it later the same day. This procedure allows the speculator a chance to profit from a one-day price fall in the option contract. The only money requirement is the *full option purchase price including commission.* He may earn a profit or he may incur a loss. This flexibility gives a speculator a chance to test his market judgment with his risk capital on the one-day direction of the price of an option—and perhaps to earn a profit.

26 Conservative Speculation through CBOE Option Spreading

The investment world (except for some truly sophisticated arbitrageurs and experienced traders) is just waking up to the fact that the Chicago Board Options Exchange has created new opportunities for seeking profits through option contracts. One of these new possibilities is the concept of *spreads*. This concept was borrowed from the commodity futures markets and adapted to CBOE options.

Currently, the most popular, attractive, and predictable CBOE option spread involves the simultaneous sale and purchase of call-option contracts on the same underlying stock. Generally, higher potential spread opportunities exist in situations where the *purchased contract has a more distant expiration month* than the one sold. The more distant month almost invariably will sell for a greater premium than the nearby month.

Registered representatives should become familiar with the entry of spread orders. Most member firms make provisions on their order tickets so that CBOE orders to sell and to buy can be entered *on a single order ticket*. An amount specified as the *spread* (which is the difference between the amount being paid for the distant month and received from the nearby month) should be indicated on a ticket. Clients entering spread orders do not have to worry about one side being executed and the other side not. The two orders are entered as a unit and *both have to be executed or no trade takes place for the client*. Of course, the order may not be executed if the client's demands are such that the market cannot fulfill them at the time. This qualification is true of all limit orders, in stock markets, and in commodity markets as well.

The client who enters into a CBOE spread situation (long the distant contract, short the nearby contract) uncollateralized by a position in the underlying stock *can never be exposed to more risk* than the amount of his spread difference *plus* his entry and exit costs.

Observe the possibilities in a spread based on the following situation. Assume that ZYX January 30s are trading at $31\frac{1}{2}$ and, at the same time, ZYX April 30s are available at 4.

An investor, knowledgeable about ZYX, observes the price differential between the two contract months and decides to enter a CBOE spread order on the stock. He instructs his broker to sell ZYX January 30s and buy ZYX April 30s with *no more than one-half point difference*. The investor is not concerned with the prices at which the orders are executed. His concern is to obtain an execution of a buy and a sell where the *spread between money received and money spent* is *no more than one-half point per contract* plus commission cost.

Let's assume that an execution is obtained with this half point differential. What then happens to the investor? His account is *credited with $350* less commissions from the sale of the ZYX January 30s call and his account is *debited $400* plus commissions from the purchase of the ZYX April call. The investor has placed at risk for each spread the cash difference of $50 plus commission expenses.

If ZYX common stock is below 30 at the end of January, the holder of the call certainly *will not call* for the stock, and the spread investor will realize $350 gross premium income. He *still owns outright* a call option on ZYX at 30 expiring in April. With ZYX under 30 (but not disastrously under), this call option with three months' life remaining will most likely have a time value between 2 and 3.

If ZYX common rises to 35 or 40 after the short call at 30 lapses, the April call option can be worth $500 to $1,000. Should ZYX common stay below 30 the entire time, the investor in the spread will lose the $50 differential between what he received and what he bought, plus his entry and exit cost. That is the *absolute dollar amount of his risk.*

Using the same facts, another possibility arises. ZYX might rise to 40 at the end of January. The spread investor then has to buy in the option he sold for $350 at a price of about $1,000. With no more time left in the option life, the value of the option is the difference between 30 and 40 (10). In closing out part of his spread, he shows a loss on that part of the transaction of approximately $650 plus the in and out cost.

However, the call he bought for 4, with three months left to run and ten points "in the money," is most likely selling for 13 or

14. He can liquidate this part of the spread now by selling the long position in the April call, thereby realizing a handsome profit after netting the two transactions.

How to Enter into a "Spread"

Registered representatives should know the different ways of entering into *fixed-risk* CBOE spreads. *Fixed risk* in CBOE spreads can only exist if the spread involves the *same underlying stock* with the *long position in the distant month hedging the short position in the nearby month.*

One way to enter a spread is naked. In option parlance, this simply means that the short call position is not collateralized by a position in the underlying stock or its equivalent in convertible securities. NYSE member firms do not currently recognize the long option as collateral for a short option. Therefore, so-called naked spreads executed with NYSE member firms must have the short call position collateralized by other securities or money. The collateral deposit required to margin spreads varies from brokerage firm to brokerage firm. It is the registered representative's responsibility to check his particular firm's requirements for these transactions.

CBOE members who are not NYSE members can, if they want, follow the margin methods allowed by the CBOE. The CBOE method allows spreads like those in our example to be considered as covered by the long call—*plus* an additional deposit equal to 10 percent of the value of the long or short position, whichever is greater.

Low-risk spreads can also exist in stable or quality investment stocks where the short call position is collateralized by the underlying securities. The investor simply deposits the stock with his broker and sells the nearby call—while simultaneously buying the distant call. The opportunity then exists for the investor to make additional profits with little more risk (the spread difference) than that in owning the underlying stock.

27 New Option-Writing Strategies for CBOE

Writing (synonymous with issuing or granting) OTC option contracts has long been ballyhooed by many put and call dealers, as well as many New York Stock Exchange member firms, as a method for conservative investors to seek high returns on capital—returns that can reach annual levels of perhaps 15 to 20 percent or more on the capital committed to option writing. The source of this hoped-for return is premiums received from option buyers. Buyers pay these premiums in return for the option writer's assumption of risk in owning the underlying stock.

Many option writers have discovered, however, that earning this return is *not an easy thing* to do. Investors and brokers alike have found out that writing options on a regular basis involves much time, detailed record keeping, frequent decision making, and wide knowledge of hundreds of different stocks that are in demand in the OTC option world. The traditional option writer has also found that there is *no simple way to defend* a position that is going against him. All these difficulties have to be *confronted, and conquered* for the OTC option writer actually to net a 15 to 20 percent return on his capital.

Moreover, he has no way of knowing whether he's writing or issuing option contracts at the best prices, or even close to the best prices, available at the time. The OTC market is a *negotiated* market. There is no price exposure and central reporting system to aid buyers and writers in comparison shopping for value. Dealers in OTC options operate on a mark-up structure rather than a commission system. Many times, these mark-ups are large and the difference between what a buyer pays for an OTC option and what the seller receives is great.

Often, no options can be issued on anything resembling a quality stock. When bids are available on quality securities, the premiums are so low that the venture is economically unfeasible for the writer.

The Chicago Board Options Exchange has provided viable solutions to many of the problems that face OTC option writers. The CBOE market has complete visibility. Through his broker, the CBOE option writer can get instant reports of high, low, last, and volume from desk-top terminals in each brokerage office. He can also check the daily CBOE option tables in the *Wall Street Journal* to see the price ranges of options he may have written or be inclined to issue. *Barron's* and *Financial Weekly* provide weekly summations of CBOE trading.

Because of the stringent listing requirements of the CBOE, the writer gets a *quality stock list to choose from,* a list that can help make his portfolio one that he can bear with.

Perhaps the *single greatest feature* of the CBOE is the *writer's ability to liquidate his position* should he so decide. This makes possible a defense and protection system that was never available in the OTC, or so-called New York, option market.

The writer on the CBOE who, typically, buys 100 shares of stock and issues a call option for any one of the various expiration months has the opportunity to relieve his obligation and eliminate his risk by simply *selling out the underlying stock* and *buying in the option* he sold previously. This secondary market liquidity feature makes possible the employment of a *prudent, risk-reducing, high profit potential strategy.*

Conservative CBOE Call Option Writing Principles

The typical CBOE call writer has *two main objectives.* One is to *protect the capital* that he has acquired. The second is to *earn a high income* from that capital. Most investing techniques normally do not offer the chance to seek both goals at the same time. CBOE call-option writing, due to its unique advantages, does present the reasonable investor the chance to fulfil his dual desires.

The covered writer of CBOE call options is entitled to retain the normal cash dividends he receives from ownership of the underlying stock, in addition to the premium he collects. His focus is on the *total return* on his capital from the dividend, premiums, and capital gains he earns from his option writing activities.

An alert eye must always be on watch for risk to his capital. The following principles will aid the writer in his profit search. The registered representative can serve his clients well by advising, and enabling, them to adhere to these guidelines.

Principle #1: Diversity

Diversification has long been a cornerstone of prudent money management. This technique should be applied to the capital committed to option writing. The maximum amount committed to any *one stock should not exceed 10 percent of the writer's capital.*

Principle #2: Calls Only

The conservative option writer should issue call contracts only. He should own the underlying stock, or securities convertible into the underlying stock. By so doing, the writer is accepting the risk of a down move in the underlying securities. This is a *risk* that can be mitigated due to the existence of a secondary market for options, a *risk* that can be defended to a great extent by employing one of several strategies.

Principle #3: Sell Distant Contract Months

The covered CBOE call writer should generally issue calls for the more distant contract months. The rationale behind this choice of expiration months is manifold. The more distant months almost invariably provide a *greater number of premium dollars,* which serves to *protect the writer's position* against a price drop. A second advantage lies in the possibility of *earning a long-term capital gain* from the premium. Also, by selling more distant contracts, *the number of investment decisions is reduced and commission expenses are substantially lower.*

Principle #4: Get at least 10% Risk Protection

All common stock investments bear risk. Some stocks are thought to be more stable and of better quality than others. Despite stability and quality, which are, perhaps, stock characteristics sought by the conservative call option writer, the premium should be large enough to permit the writer to *earn an annual return of at least 20 percent.* At the same time, since *profit has a limit* and *risk is incurred, protection* in the form of premium dollars *should approach 10 percent* of the writer's commitment to make the venture economically feasible.

Principle #5: Protect Capital

A timeworn axiom oft quoted to investors by the so-called wise men of Wall Street is, "Cut your losses short; let your profits run." This advice has proven difficult for brokers and investors to follow. At what point should losses be cut? Exact guidelines are difficult both to come by and adhere to. Losses are generally an anathema to most investors.

Prudent call writers, however, should *plan a conservative program* upon entry into the option-writing world. This program should deal with the handling of covered calls when a stock decline is being experienced. *The covered writer earns money on any stock that rises, stays even,* or *goes down less than the premium received.* His one worry is a stock price decline greater than the premium received.

One capital protection method that the registered representative can present to an investor is to *suggest the sale of the underlying stock when a decline has eradicated the bulk of protection afforded by the advance premium.* Simultaneous with the sale of the stock, a call should be purchased (with the same strike and expiration as the one previously sold) to eliminate the writer's obligation.

This procedure normally offsets the loss on the stock sale, to a large extent, with the profit from closing the call obligation. The writer's capital is recovered relatively intact and is available for reinvestment.

Another capital conserving method can be used to defend a sinking stock position. Should a stock drop to a level where the bulk of the call premium has been lost, the call option writer may be able to buy a call (with the same terms as the one issued) and earn a profit. Generally, *call options drop in value as the underlying stock declines and as time evaporates.* The profit the writer earns may offset the paper loss in the underlying stock he still holds. Upon buying the call and closing out his obligation, the writer may be able to issue a call on the same stock with a *more distant expiration* month, thereby enabling him to take in more premium dollars to cushion his stock position loss.

This method, of course, can only be used if a more distant month has been admitted to trading after the first call has been issued. It does offer the advantage of avoiding the commission expenses of selling the underlying stock and provides more down-side protection for the CBOE call writer.

Summing Up

If a covered CBOE call option writer follows the foregoing guidelines, he will find himself in this position. He is earning premium dollars on any stock that experiences a price rise. He is earning premium dollars on any stock that remains at, or around, the purchase price. He is earning premium dollars on any stock that declines less than the premium he collects. He continues to collect and retain all cash dividends received.

By employing some of the preceding defenses, the writer can hope to break approximately even on stocks that experience sharp declines, because the loss he incurs on selling out the stock will, hopefully, be offset to a great extent by the profit he earns from purchasing his call option obligation.

These principles *can help to reduce option-writing risk to a minimum.* Those who follow them have an excellent opportunity to earn returns of 15 to 20 percent or more annually on their option-writing capital.

Hedge option writing, as detailed in Chapter 14, is a viable money management technique use by aggressive, informed CBOE option writers. These writers tend to write partially covered calls. Sometimes they may buy 100 shares and issue two or more calls. When the *market price of the stock is far below the exercise price*, the aggressive writers tend to increase the number of calls issued per 100 shares of stock in their inventory.

PARTIAL HEDGE EXAMPLE. In December 1973, ZYX April 70's were trading at 7. ZYX stock was at 63. A hedge writer buys 100 ZYX at 63, and he sells two *ZYX, April 70 calls at 7 each.* The $1,400 premium protects the 100 shares bought at 63 to the level of $49 should the stock be below 70 at the end of April. If the stock rises above 70, the writer will not be at any real capital risk until the level of 91 is reached.

He establishes a profit zone ranging from 49 to 91. If the stock remains between those parameters, he will earn a profit. The 91 up-side parameter is computed by adding to the 70 strike price, the $1,400 premium, and the $700 gain from the 100 shares bought at 63 and to be delivered at 70. (Commissions are excluded to simplify.)

Should either action point (49 or 71) be penetrated, a defense can be employed as outlined in Chapters 14, 15, and 16. The prime goals of hedge option writers are the very high rate of return and maximum protection of capital, combined with a knowledge of, but lack of concern for, the tax consequences of short-term gains.

28 CBOE Option Contract Adjustments

Registered representatives who intend to buy or sell Chicago Board Options Exchange contracts should be well acquainted with how these contracts are adjusted when cash dividends, stock dividends, stock splits, rights, and warrants are issued by the underlying company. Some of the adjustments are significantly different from the adjustments to OTC option contracts.

Cash dividends do not reduce the striking price of CBOE option contracts. This characteristic differs sharply from the OTC option, in which cash dividends *do reduce* the striking price. This very important difference *makes writing CBOE contracts very attractive* for many knowledgeable, quality option writers. There is an exception, however, when the cash dividend being distributed represents a return of capital dividend for tax purposes. If a cash return of capital dividend occurs in a stock underlying the CBOE option contract, the striking price is reduced by the amount down to the nearest one-eighth per share.

Stock dividends, stock splits, and *reverse splits* on stocks underlying CBOE contracts require adjustment of two fundamental terms of CBOE open positions on the ex date. Both the number of shares under the option (which is initially set at 100) and the exercise price are adjusted by applying special formulas devised by the CBOE.[1]

Rights, warrants, and spin-offs, if issued by a company whose stock underlies the CBOE option, necessitate an adjustment in CBOE open contracts. This adjustment will reflect the spin-off securities, rights, or warrants. However, if rights or warrants being issued by the company *will expire prior to the expiration* of an option contract on the underlying stock, a cash adjustment is made to reflect the value of these ex rights or ex warrants on their ex date. The exercise prices of open positions affected by these distributions *is reduced.*

[1] See *Managing Customer Accounts on the Chicago Board Options Exchange* (Chicago, Ill.: Chicago Board Options Exchange, 1973), p. 66.

The CBOE intends to *start a new class of option contracts when a substantial price change* occurs in the underlying stock. On stocks priced over $100, new classes of contracts will be started when the stock price moves upward about 20 points or down 10 points.

On stocks priced under $100 but over $50, new classes generally will be started on price rises of 10 points. The new classes are started to make the contracts' striking prices approximate the underlying price of the stock. On stocks priced under $50, new exercise prices will begin when five-point moves have taken place in the underlying stock. When new classes are started, the old contract classes still continue to be available for trading until expiration.

29 Option Tax Treatment and Tax Strategies

Although the registered representative is not a licensed tax advisor, he should know certain basic tax treatments concerning premiums paid by option buyers and received by option writers. Additional knowledge concerning option tax strategy may prove very helpful to account executives in obtaining and retaining clients.

Current Option Tax Treatment of Premiums, Paid by Option Buyers

Call Options

If a call option buyer elects to exercise his privilege, he adds *the premium he originally paid* to the cost of the stock being bought through the exercise of his call. The resulting figure becomes his cost basis for tax purposes. Please note that *the holding period for the stock bought through exercise of a call begins with the date the call is exercised, not the date the call option was purchased!*

If a call option is bought, held for a period longer than six months, *and then* sold, any profit earned on the transaction will be taxed as a *long-term capital gain.* For maximum after-tax gains, it is imperative that call option owners be aware of the *difference in tax consequences between exercising an option and selling an option.*

For example, assume that a six-month, ten-day call is bought January 1 on stock XYZ at 40, for a $500 premium. The call is then sold July 3 on XYZ at 40 with the stock price at 50 for $1,000. Deduct $500 as the premium cost, and the long-term profit is $500 (commissions excluded to simplify).

Under present tax rules, short-term losses can be more valuable to investors than long-term losses. For this reason, the following *tax strategy should be firmly established* as part of an option investor's money management program.

Assume that an option buyer purchases an over-six-month

option and believes at the end of five months and twenty-nine days *that the option is likely to expire worthless* due to an adverse move in the underlying stock. He can *sell the apparently worthless option for a nominal amount* ($1.00 is quite often the figure), either to an option dealer, a NYSE member firm who has an option department, or on the CBOE, if the option trades there. By so doing, the investor *establishes a short-term loss* for tax purposes on an option bought originally in search of a long-term gain.

If a call option *expires,* the holder of the call is entitled to claim the premium loss as a capital loss. The loss can be either short term or long term, depending how long the call option was held.

CONVERTING SHORT-TERM GAINS INTO LONG-TERM GAINS. This strategy can potentially create a long-term gain for a call option buyer who has a short-term gain situation to work with. Assume that on January 2 an investor purchases a six-month, ten-day call option on ZYX at 20 for a premium cost of $300. On April 2, ZYX stock is selling for $30 per share. The investor is delighted with the short-term, paper gain and with his correct judgment. If his profit were long term, he would sell his option and realize his gain.

The option informed broker can suggest *freezing* the gain in an attempt to convert the short-term gain into a long-term gain in this way.

Step 1: On April 2, have the client "short" 100 ZYX at 30 (assuming the stock can be borrowed and the client can collateralize the short sale).

Step 2: On July 12 (or any day after six months but before lapse of the call), if the stock is above 30 (at 40, for example), sell the call option for its full value. Using 40 as the market price of the stock on July 12, the call can be sold for $2,000 (commissions omitted to simplify). This leaves the investor with a $1,700 *long-term gain* after deducting the premium expense of $300.

Step 3: On July 12, buy 100 ZYX at 40 to cover the short sale made at 30. This will create a $1,000 *short-term loss.* After netting the two transactions, the client has $700 as a *long-term gain.*

Please note: *If ZYX were 20 on July 3, the call would be valueless.* The short sale at 30 would be covered by buying 100 ZYX at 20 and using that stock to close the short sale. The gain on the closing of the short sale would be a $1,000 short-term gain. After netting the option loss against the short sale gain, the investor would still benefit by $700.

Put Options

If a put option buyer elects to exercise his privilege to sell stock, he subtracts the premium paid for the put from the proceeds of the sale. From the result (put price less premium paid) he deducts the cost of the stock being delivered via the put exercise.

Any gain earned on a put option held for more than six months and then sold (not exercised) is treated as a *long-term capital gain.* This is the *only way* a long-term capital gain can be earned *from a stock price decline!*

If a put option *expires,* the holder of the put is entitled to claim the premium loss as a capital loss. The loss can be long term or short term depending on how long the put is held.

Warning: A put cannot be acquired and utilized in an attempt to convert a short-term gain in a stock into a long-term gain in the stock. Acquisition of a put is considered to *interrupt* the holding period of stock owned less than six months.

For example, suppose 100 ZYX is bought January 1 at 20. A put on ZYX is bought June 1 at a striking price of 30. In this situation, an inexperienced investor might want to freeze the profit at the 30 level and, on July 2, exercise the put and deliver the stock held more than six months, thereby establishing a long-term gain. *This practice is not allowed.*

PUT INSURANCE. An investor who seeks a profit in a volatile stock but fears a big loss can buy the stock and buy a put on that same stock on the same day. During the put time period, *he can lose no more than his put premium and commission expenses.*

If the put is identified as insurance for the stock bought, the cost of the put is added to the cost of the stock to determine the tax basis for the stock. Should the stock rise substantially and be sold after a six-month holding period, a long-term capital gain can be earned. Should the stock decline substantially, the put can be exercised, thereby holding the loss to the put cost plus commissions.

The registered representative as well as option investors should know that the foregoing strategy is seldom used, since unlimited gain potential and fixed risk limit can be obtained by simply buying a call option.

Straddle buyers must allocate their straddle premium cost on a consistent and uniform basis. The suggested allocation is 55 percent to the call and 45 percent to the put. However, other supportable regular allocation percentages would probably be allowed. After allocation, the tax treatment and strategies as detailed above would come into play.

Current Tax Treatment of Premiums Paid to Option Writers

Call Options

If an issued call option is not exercised, the premium is treated as *ordinary income in the year the option expires*. If an issued call option is exercised, the premium received is added to the price of the stock being delivered. The writer then subtracts from the sale price plus the premium the cost of the stock being delivered. The resulting figure determines the capital gain or loss. The gain or loss can be either short or long term, based on the holding period of the stock used to meet the call.

Put Options

If an issued put option *is not exercised,* the premium received is treated as ordinary income in the year the put option expires. If the put option is exercised, the premium received is *used to reduce the purchase price of the stock bought* through the put exercise.

Straddle Options

Under present IRS rules, option writers allocate between the put and the call the premium received. The suggested allocation is 55 percent to the call and 45 percent to the put. However, any supportable consistent allocation would generally be allowed.

Once the straddle writer has made his allocation, *any gain from a portion of the straddle that lapses is treated as a short-term capital gain. This is true even if a straddle is issued for longer than six months.*

The gain or loss on the part of the straddle that is exercised is treated as outlined in the first and second paragraphs of this section.

RISK REDUCTION AND POSSIBLE CONVERSION OF SHORT-TERM GAINS INTO LONG-TERM GAINS. The following tax strategy can be valuable to option writers. Assume that on January 1 an investor buys 100 ZYX at 20. On May 1, ZYX is 30, and the investor would like to "insure" some of his profit and perhaps earn a long-term capital gain. He can sell a 65-day call expiring July 6 for $250. If ZYX is over 30 on July 6, he most likely will be called. Upon exercise, the call premium of $250 is added to the sale price at 30 to determine his total sales price. After deducting his purchase price of 20, he will have *a long-term gain of $1,250,* as he will have delivered stock held over six months (commissions excluded to simplify).

Please note the premium attaches to the holding period of the stock being delivered. If the stock is under 30 on July 6, the writer earns the $250 premium through lapse of the option and can then decide whether to sell the stock or write another call.

CONVERTING SHORT-TERM GAINS INTO LONG-TERM GAINS. Assume the following facts. An option writer has realized a short gain of $5,000 by March 1. On March 2, he buys 500 ZYX at 20 and writes five six-month, ten-day calls at 20 for $300 each. On October 12, ZYX is 33. This is the last day of the option's life and *the writer knows the calls* will be exercised. If he takes no other action, he will be called out of 500 ZYX at 20 and will have earned $1,500 (5 × $300) long-term gain (before commission expenses) to go with his previously earned $5,000 short-term gain.

If he or his registered representative are option knowledgeable, he might employ the following strategy. On October 12, the writer can sell the 500 ZYX at 33 versus the purchase at 20. *This would establish clearly a $6,500 long-term gain* (commissions excluded).

The writer can then immediately purchase (no wash sale rule violation) 500 ZYX at 33 and earmark those shares for delivery at 20 against the calls being exercised that day at 20. *Upon exercise of the calls that day, he shows a $5,000 short-term loss.*

October 12	Bought	500 ZXY at 33	=	$16,500
October 12	Sold	500 ZXY at 23	=	−$11,500
		(20 + $300 premium loss)	=	$ 5,000

The $5,000, short-term one-day loss can be applied against the $5,000, short-term gains taken earlier. This leaves the writer with $6,500 net long-term gain!

CALL WRITING STRATEGY AGAINST LOW COST BASIS STOCK. Frequently, an investor will be attracted to call option writing for the immediate cash flow that option writing produces. The investor may have a diversified portfolio of low cost basis common stocks that offer little in the way of current income. For estate and tax purposes, he may want to continue to own the stocks. At the same time, he may desire more income dollars to meet the rising cost of living. This investor might hesitate to embark on a call-writing program that utilized his low cost basis stocks for fear that he might be called and forced to pay a substantial capital gains tax upon delivering his lost cost stock.

The option informed registered representative can allay the

fears of the low cost basis investor by explaining that *a call is not against any specific hundred shares of stock!* Upon exercise of a call, the obligation can be fulfilled by delivering any hundred shares of the stock being called.

Assume the following facts. An investor owns 100 ZYX with a cost basis of 1. ZYX is now selling at 50, and the investor writes a six-month call for a premium of $650. If the stock is below 50 at expiration, the call will expire and the investor will have happily earned his $650. He will still have possession of his low cost stock, which he *never* intended to sell. His income has been substantially enhanced through writing the call.

If, at expiration, the stock is at 60 (or higher), knowing that the call will be exercised and *not wishing* to deliver his low cost stock, the investor can instruct his broker to buy 100 ZYX at 60 and identify it as stock to be delivered against the call being exercised at 50.

Bought (new)	100 ZYX at 60 =	$6,000
Sold	100 ZYX at	$5,650 (50 plus $650 call premium received)
	Short-term loss =	$350[a] plus commission expenses

[a] Fully deductible against ordinary income up to $1,000

The short-term, tax deductible loss is offset by the greater value (60) of his low cost basis ZYX.

The tax treatment and strategies presented in this chapter apply both to CBOE and OTC option contracts.

Glossary

ARBITRAGE: The simultaneous purchase and sale of securities in different markets to seek profits through price disparities between the markets.

AVERAGING: The practice of buying or selling the same security at different prices. Buying more, higher, is known as *averaging up*. Buying more, lower, is known as *averaging down*.

AUCTION MARKET: A market in which sales result from competing bids and offers rather than from posted prices.

BUY-STOP ORDER: A contingent order entered by a client instructing the broker to buy at the market when and if a stock sells at or above a specified price.

BEARISH OPTION WRITER: A call option grantor who has no position in the stock underlying the call, or who is short the stock underlying a put. He takes the risk that the stock may rise.

BULLISH OPTION WRITER: An option issuer who collateralizes calls with a position in the stock (or its equivalent) and collateralizes puts backed with cash or its equivalent. He takes the risk that the stock may fall.

CALL OPTION (OTC): The right to buy 100 shares of a specified stock at a fixed price for a set period of time. Upon exercise, and according to the terms, this contract may be adjusted for stock splits, stock dividends, rights, warrants, cash dividends, and mergers.

CBOE: An abbreviation for the Chicago Board Options Exchange.

COLLATERAL: Money, bonds, or stocks pledged to a broker to secure a loan.

COVER: A term generally used in connection with short sales to indicate the closing of the short sale either by buying the securities sold short or delivering their equivalent in convertible securities.

DEBIT BALANCE: The amount borrowed from the brokerage firm by a client to finance margin account transactions.

DOLLAR COST AVERAGE: An investment process involving the periodic investing of relatively equal amounts of money over a time period.

ENDORSE: A term meaning guarantee. An NYSE member firm assures the buyer of an option that the *firm* will honor the terms of the contract. Even if a writer fails in his obligation, the firm will make good as per the terms of the contract.

ENDORSEMENT FEE: A sum paid by put and call dealers to New York Stock Exchange member firms to endorse (guarantee performance) option contracts for the client of the member firm. This fee generally ranges from $6.25 to $25 per option.

EQUITY: The investor's ownership interest in the account (or security); the amount that would be left if all debts and claims against the account (or security) were satisfied.

EXECUTION: The consummation of a transaction to buy or sell.

EXPIRATION DATE: The last day on which an option can be exercised.

FIRM: An option-world term used to indicate a commitment to buy or sell a stated number of contracts for an agreed-upon premium.

HOUSE: The brokerage firm.

INITIAL MARGIN: The amount of dollars, in cash or in loan value of securities, a client is required by law (Regulation T of the Securities Exchange Act of 1934) to deposit on purchases made in his margin account.

LAPSED OPTION: A put contract or a call contract that has expired unexercised.

LEVERAGE: The use of borrowed money that is added to the client's equity in order to increase the profit potential of a transaction. It also increases the loss potential.

LIMIT ORDER: A buy or sell order at a fixed price.

LIQUIDATION: A Wall Street term to denote the changing of securities into cash.

LOAN CONSENT: An agreement requested of margin clients that permits the broker to temporarily lend the securities in the account to short sellers or other brokers to facilitate settlement of transactions. Such loans are fully protected by cash collateral.

LONG OPTION: A put contract or call contract owned by an investor.

MARGIN AGREEMENT: The agreement required of a margin client that permits the broker both to use securities in the margin account as collateral for brokers' loans and to sell securities, if necessary, to protect the money loaned to the client.

MAINTENANCE MARGIN: The minimum level to which a client's equity may decline before he will have to deposit additional cash or securities.

NAKED OPTION WRITER: An option grantor who sells calls without owning the underlying stock, or puts without being short the stock.

NEW ISSUE (OR PRIMARY ISSUE): A new security that is issued by a corporation under the Securities Act of 1933 and sold for the first time.

OTC (OVER-THE-COUNTER): A marketplace where trades are negotiated.

OPTION WRITING: The practice of issuing call contracts and put contracts with guaranteed fixed stock prices in return for advance dollar premiums.

REGISTERED REPRESENTATIVE: A term used by the NYSE, ASE, and NASD to identify employees of members who have met the qualification requirements necessary to permit solicitation of orders and client accounts for their firms.

RIGHTS: Securities issued by companies entitling shareholders to buy new securities. The rights issued are based on the number of shares owned and usually offer the shareholders the opportunity to invest more money at a price lower than that available to nonshareholders.

RISKLESS SHORT SALE: A sale of securities *protected completely* by a call option entitling the owner to buy the securities necessary to cover the short. If the short sale is executed at a price above the exercise price, to allow the locking in of premium recovery and commission expense, the short holds no capital risk for the investor.

SELL OUT: The sale of a customer's securities after his failure to deposit additional collateral to protect the broker's loan to him. This usually occurs under adverse market conditions.

SELL STOP: An order given to a broker (NYSE member) instructing him to sell a specific number of shares at the market price as soon as a transaction has occurred at the sell-stop price. Orders of this type may be suspended at certain times by the NYSE.

SHORT AGAINST THE BOX: A sale of securities when a like amount is owned in the account but will be delivered at a later date. This practice is used generally to postpone taxes on security profits.

SHORT OPTION: An option (not owned) issued (put or call) by an option writer.

SHORT SALE (REGULAR): A sale of securities *not owned.* (Securities sold short are normally borrowed from the investor's broker.) At some later date, the securities sold short must be replaced. If bought lower, a profit results; if higher, a loss is incurred.

SPECIAL OPTION: A put or call contract that has previously been issued and the terms have been established. Special options generally have strike prices away from the current market price. Most dealers' special options are for short time periods.

SPREAD (CBOE): Dual transactions effected on the CBOE involving the purchase of a contract and the sale of a contract at a specified price difference between the two executions.

SPREAD (OTC): An option combination consisting of one call option and one put option. Generally at initiation the striking price in the call is higher than the market price of the stock, and the striking price in the put is lower than the market price of the stock.

STOCK SPLIT: An increase in the number of outstanding shares of a company effected by distributing shares to each stockholder on a basis so that a stockholder's *ratio* of equity in the company is unchanged.

STRAP: An option combination consisting of two call options and one put option all with the same strike price and expiration date.

STRIP: An option combination consisting of two put options and one call option all with the same strike price and expiration date.

STRIKE PRICE: The price specified in the option contract at which the option may be exercised (subject to adjustments according to the terms of the contract).

SYNDICATE: An investment banking combine that bands together to underwrite and distribute new security issues or secondary sales of large blocks of stocks or bonds.

TAX EXEMPT: A term applied to municipal bonds whose interest payments are free (exempt) from federal income taxes.

UPTICK: A price higher than the last price.

WARRANT: A certificate issued by a company giving the holder the right to buy securities at a set price. Some warrants have time limits and some are perpetual.

WARRANT HEDGE: The practice of selling stock short protected by a long position in warrants entitling the holder to acquire (generally upon payment of money) the stock sold short.

WHIPSAW: A sharp price move in a stock followed by a quick price reversal.

WRITE: A term used in the option world that is meant to be synonymous with *issue* or *grant*.

ZERO UPTICK: A price the same as the last price but higher than the last preceding different price.